Parallel Programming

A New Approach

Parallel Programming
A New Approach

Michael H. Coffin
University of Waterloo

Silicon Press
Summit, NJ 07901, USA

Printing 9 8 7 6 5 4 3 2 1   Year 96 95 94 93 92

Library of Congress Cataloging-in-Publication Data

Coffin, Michael H.
  Parallel Programming : A New Approach / Coffin, Michael H.
    p. cm.
  ISBN 0-929306-13-9
  1. Parallel Programming (Computer science) I. Title
  QA76.642.C64   1992   91-46845
  004´.35--dc20   CIP

Contents

List of Figures

Preface

Electronic computers were introduced into general use in the early nineteen fifties. These early computers were much faster than human or mechanical calculators, but not fast enough to satisfy their users. Although modern computers are many orders of magnitude faster than early ones, the need for even more speed persists. Large problems in engineering, physics, mathematics, and artificial intelligence tax even the fastest computers currently available.

However, the speed of sequential (von Neumann) computers is limited by a fundamental physical law: signals cannot propagate faster than the speed of light. Modern sequential computers are approaching that limit. This has led hardware designers and manufacturers to build parallel computers having more than one independent processing element. Parallel computers overcome the fundamental limit on calculation speed imposed by the speed of light by performing many calculations simultaneously. Currently, the fastest computers in the world are parallel computers.

As is often the case, however, software design lags hardware design. Out of concern for speed, programs for parallel computers are often written in extremely low-level languages. This results in parallel programs that are, perhaps, efficient on a particular parallel computer. Unfortunately, such programs are also difficult to write, difficult to read, and often depend so strongly on the capabilities of a particular computer that they are almost impossible to move to other—even fairly similar—computers. The situation is somewhat as it was in the early days of sequential programming, before the advent of high-level languages.

This book addresses the problem of how to write parallel programs that are simultaneously portable, efficient, and clearly written. All these aspects are essential. Portability is important because rewriting programs for different architectures is expensive and prone to error. Efficiency is important because the main reason for using parallel computers is speed; inefficient programs squander the expensive resources provided by parallel computers. Clarity is important in all programming; unclear programs are hard to write, hard to maintain, and are apt to be erroneous.

The method presented in this book begins with a statement of the algorithm in a clear, straightforward style; at this stage messy architectural details are ignored. The program is then refined by adding scheduling and mapping annotations, which specialize the algorithm to the target architecture. The annotations are separated syntactically from the statement of the algorithm so they do not obscure the algorithm and so they can easily be changed, if necessary, for other target architectures. The original statement of the algorithm is not changed.

Using annotations to achieve efficiency allows programs to be written in a highly architecture-independent way while still allowing complete control over details of the calculation when necessary. Programs can be tested for correctness before annotations are added since annotations are not required for correctness. The use of annotations also allows programs to be tailored to various architectures without changing the basic (unannotated) program. This allows various strategies for scheduling and mapping to be tried without affecting the correctness of a program.

The idea of using refinement to develop programs is not new; neither is the use of annotations to control parallelism. (Some other approaches that employ refinement and annotations are discussed in Section 6.9.) However, we believe that the method presented in this book significantly generalizes and extends previous approaches, allowing the programmer to exert precise control over scheduling and data placement without adding complexity to the original parallel algorithm.

Acknowledgements. I am indebted to many people for discussions and comments on the work presented in this book. First, without the help of Greg Andrews, my PhD supervisor, the dissertation upon which this book is based could never have been written. I am also grateful to Peter Downey, Norm Hutchinson, Ron Olsson, and Rick Schlichting for many valuable comments, criticisms, and suggestions.

Chapter 1

Introduction

Ideally, programs for parallel computers should be portable, efficient, and clearly written. Any one of these objectives can easily be met. Portability and clarity can be achieved by writing programs in very-high-level languages. Unfortunately, current compilers cannot be relied upon to produce efficient object code for such programs. Efficiency can be achieved by writing programs in assembly language, but assembly language programs are not portable and are not as clear as programs written in higher-level languages. The difficulty lies in achieving all three goals simultaneously.

The chief obstacle to writing parallel programs that are simultaneously portable and efficient is the diversity of parallel computers. Portability between sequential architectures has been achieved largely because modern sequential computers are remarkably similar. Although sequential computers differ in details such as number of registers, addressing modes, and cache sizes, the differences between various sequential computers can be hidden from the programmer by a relatively thin layer of abstraction. For example, the C programming language [69], which is a very low-level language, can be implemented efficiently on almost all modern sequential computers. This is possible because details such as how to utilize registers and the choice of addressing modes are ignored by the C language and are provided automatically by C compilers.

The same is not true of parallel computers, which differ in ways that cannot be disguised by such a thin layer of abstraction. Our focus in this book is on the most flexible and common kind of parallel computer: the multiple-instruction, multiple-data (MIMD) computer. MIMD computers differ in the number of processors, memory organization, interconnection topology, minimum efficient task size, and other aspects of their architecture. The number of processors can range over several orders of magnitude, from two to tens of thousands. The memory can be shared and equally accessible to all the processors (*uniform memory access*, or UMA), it can be shared but with non-uniform access times (*non-uniform memory access*, or NUMA), or it can be distributed among the processors. Distributed-memory computers can have interconnection networks that are arranged as rings, grids, hypercubes, trees, or other configurations. The minimum efficient task size (the *granularity*) of parallel computers varies from one instruction to hundreds. In addition, some computers have hardware support for locks, semaphores, message passing, or other synchronization and communication primitives. These differences can profoundly affect the way calculations are organized for efficient execution.

The chief obstacle to writing programs that are simultaneously clear, and efficient is the complexity of parallel computers. Von Neumann computers have a single processor and a single memory module; all calculation must take place on the processor and all data must be stored in the memory module. Parallel computers can have many processors and memory modules, and the processors can be connected by complicated networks. To specify a parallel calculation it is necessary to specify which calculations take place on each processor, which data is assigned to each memory module, and how the communication network is utilized for communication and synchronization. The way these details are specified is often important to the efficiency of the calculation. The way tasks are assigned to processors affects processor utilization; if too few tasks are assigned to a processor it will be idle during part of the calculation. The way data are assigned to memory modules affects the speed with which processors access data and thus the speed of calculation. The choice of communication paths between processors affects the time required for communication and synchronization.

The rest of this chapter outlines a spectrum of possible approaches to parallel programming and then introduces the Par approach, which is the subject of this book.

1.1 Approaches

Any language for parallel computation on MIMD computers must accomplish several things:

- First, parallelism must be found. We call the natural units of parallelism in an algorithm *chores*. For explicitly parallel languages finding chores is trivial since parallelism is specified directly. For languages without explicit parallelism, finding chores can be a major problem. Section 6.1 discusses some of the pitfalls of deriving parallel code from sequential programs.

- Second, the parallelism must be tailored to fit the target computer. Too little parallelism will result in idle processors; too much parallelism can result in slowdown instead of speedup because of the multiprogramming overhead that is incurred when many small tasks are executed on a processor. Thus it is often necessary to combine small chores into larger tasks suitable for the target computer.

- Third, the tasks must be assigned to processors. The best way to assign tasks to processors depends, in general, on both the structure of the computation and the topology of the interconnection network that connects the processors. For some parallel algorithms, static assignment is appropriate; for others, dynamic scheduling is needed.

- Finally, since the tasks of a program usually are not entirely independent, a language for parallel computation must provide ways for tasks to communicate and synchronize.

Languages for parallel computation differ greatly in the degree to which these steps are automated. At one extreme are parallelizing compilers, which attempt to do everything automatically. These languages offer a high degree of portability since the code does not address architectural details at all. However, the approach is only successful to the extent that the compiler and run-time system can fill in the computational details missing from the program. Unfortunately, this is difficult to do well. All the steps outlined in the previous paragraph are fundamentally difficult. Compilers cannot hope to obtain optimum solutions except in trivial cases, and even approximate solutions can require a prohibitive amount of work.

For example, a common problem with parallelizing compilers is that a program that appears as if it should be efficient executes much too slowly. This can happen, for example, if the compiler fails to find the parallelism inherent in the program or if it assigns a datum to the "wrong" memory module, resulting in many expensive references to that datum. It can be difficult or impossible to fix such performance bugs since it is difficult to decide what has gone wrong and even more difficult to modify the program so that the problem does not occur. The former problem arises because parallelizing compilers radically restructure programs, making any kind of debugging difficult. The latter problem arises because the model of computation does not contain the concept of parallelism or of a memory module; thus the language provides no way to specify parallelism directly or to force the datum to be stored in the right place. The difficulties encountered in parallelizing compilers are explored further in Sections 6.1 and 6.2.

At the other extreme are languages tailored to particular architectures or classes of architectures; for example, distributed languages are tailored specifically for distributed computers. These languages allow highly efficient programs to be written since most of the details of the calculation are explicitly specified in the program. However, such programs are non-portable, both because they are specified in terms of the architectural details of a particular computer and because they cannot utilize architectural features of other computers. For example, programs written in distributed languages may rely on the availability of a fixed number of processors, and they cannot make efficient use of shared memory since the programming model does not allow objects to be shared between processors. Parallel programs written in such languages tend also to be unclear; the large number of details required to specify the calculation tends to obscure the meaning of the algorithm.

Between the two extremes are languages that hide some details from the programmer but expose others. For example, a language may have explicit constructs to specify parallelism but hide the fact that memory access is not uniform; a compiler for such a language would automatically assign data to memory modules. Hiding details from the programmer tends to make programs less efficient but clearer and more portable. Some languages of this type are described in Chapter 6.

Another approach to parallel programming, quite different from those described above, is the annotational approach. The idea behind the annotational approach is to begin with a clear statement of the algorithm and add annotations to specify details that are necessary for efficient execution. In principle, annotations can be added to any language. Compiler directives (pragmas), for example, are a primitive form of annotation. Several parallel programming languages that support annotations are described in Chapter 6. The Par approach uses annotations.

1.2   Outline of the Par Approach

The Par approach to parallel programming begins with a statement of the algorithm in an explicitly parallel, imperative language. This initial program is written in a clear, straightforward style; at this stage messy architectural details are ignored. Explicit parallelism is used because parallel programs more closely mirror parallel algorithms than do sequential programs; thus a parallel program is a clearer expression of a parallel algorithm than is a sequential program.

The program is then refined by adding scheduling and mapping annotations, which specialize the algorithm to the target architecture. Scheduling annotations specify how chores are assigned to processors; mapping annotations specify how data is stored in memory. The annotations are separated syntactically from the statement of the algorithm so that they do not obscure the algorithm and so that they can easily be changed, if necessary, for other target architectures. The original statement of the algorithm is not changed.

The implementation of the annotations is done in the same language as the rest of the program. Thus the programmer is not restricted to a fixed set of annotations or to fixed implementations of existing annotations. Instead, the annotations can, if necessary, be tailored precisely to a specific program and computer architecture. However, it is anticipated that implementations of schedulers and mappings are good candidates for code reuse since they often depend more on the architecture than on the specific application.

Adding correctly implemented annotations to a program does not affect the correctness of the program. This makes it easy to experiment with different scheduling and mapping strategies without introducing errors. Conversely, the meaning of a program does not depend on the way it is annotated; this makes it easier to understand a program or prove it correct.

In more detail, the Par approach consists of the following steps.

1. Pick a parallel algorithm.

2. Write a program that is a clean, direct statement of the algorithm, without regard for the target architecture. Use abstract data types in declarations. Express concurrency explicitly and in units natural to the algorithm (*chores*).

3. Add scheduling annotations to cluster chores into tasks (units of parallelism that can be efficiently implemented) and assign tasks to processors.

4. Add mapping annotations to ensure that data references in tasks are (at least mostly) local to the processor to which the task has been assigned.

5. Annotate abstract data types with concrete data types that implement the necessary mappings.

6. If necessary, provide implementations of the schedulers and concrete data types that are used.

After the first two steps are complete, the program can be compiled and executed. The other steps are needed to make the program run efficiently. The annotations of steps 3, 4, and 5 augment the algorithm but do not change it.

Step 6 should be necessary only occasionally since we anticipate that schedulers and mappings will usually be taken from a library tailored to a specific computer. Chapters 3 and 4 contain many examples of general-purpose schedulers and mappings.

1.3 An Example

Consider the problem of adding two vectors of real numbers and assigning the result to a third vector. The straightforward parallel algorithm is to add the vector elements in parallel. In the Par language (which is described in Chapter 2), this is expressed as follows:

```
program add
    n : 100
    a, b, result : Vector⟨Real⟩(1, n)
    co i := 1 to n →
        result[i] := a[i] + b[i]
    oc
end add
```

The first line of the program declares n to be the constant 100. The next line declares three vectors of real elements, each indexed from 1 to n. The concurrent (**co** ... **oc**) statement specifies concurrent execution of its body.   Each instance of the body is

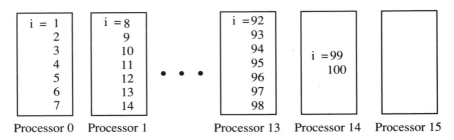

Figure 1.1: The effect of the scheduler **block**.

called a *chore*. The above concurrent statement specifies n chores, each consisting of an addition and an assignment, to be done in parallel.

This accomplishes the first two steps in our method. The program closely mirrors the parallel algorithm. The parallelism is expressed explicitly and without regard for architectural details such as the number of processors or the network topology. The vectors are shared among the parallel chores without regard for the memory organization. The above program is complete and could be compiled by a Par compiler and then executed.

The next step is to annotate the concurrent statement to specify the way chores are combined into tasks and assigned to processors. This is done for purposes of efficiency. For example, if p processors are available, with $p < n$, the n chores can be combined into tasks, each of which will contain approximately n/p chores. Each processor will then execute a single task. The Par library contains a scheduler named **block**, which implements this partitioning strategy. The effect is shown schematically in Figure 1.1 for the case where $n = 100$ and $p = 16$.   (Since 100 is not a multiple of 16 the chores do not divide evenly among the processors; processor 14 will execute only 2 chores and processor 15 will not execute any. However, the maximum number of chores per processor is 7, which is the minimum that can be achieved for any partition of the chores.)

To use the scheduler **block**, a scheduling annotation is added to the concurrent statement as follows:

```
program add
    n : 100
    a, b, result : Vector⟨Real⟩(1, n)
    co i := 1 to n {scheduler block} →
        result[i] := a[i] + b[i]
    oc
end add
```

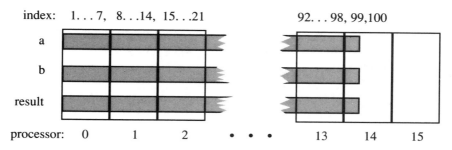

index: 1...7, 8...14, 15...21   92...98, 99,100

a

b

result

processor: 0   1   2   • • •   13   14   15

Figure 1.2: The effect of the mapping block

The way schedulers are constructed is discussed in Section 2.10.2. Notice, however, that to apply a scheduler such as block it is not necessary to know the details of how it is implemented; it suffices to know the way it partitions the chores.

With the addition of the scheduling annotation, the program now specifies a task for each processor. The next step is to annotate the code to ensure that at least most of the data resides on the processor that will access it. Since nonlocal access to data is expensive on many parallel computers, programs that employ nonlocal access will not execute efficiently on those computers. Mapping annotations are used to specify how data is placed in memory. To ensure that access to the vectors is local, the mappings of the three vectors must mirror the scheduler block. That is, the ith element of each vector must map to the same processor as does the ith chore. The standard mapping block, shown schematically in Figure 1.2, does exactly that; hence:

```
program add
    n : 100
    a, b, result : Vector⟨Real⟩(1, n)
    {map a, b, result : block}
    co i := 1 to n {scheduler block} →
        result[i] := a[i] + b[i]
    oc
end add
```

Again, explanation of the way mappings are constructed is left until later; for now the mapping block is regarded as a specification that each processor "owns" a segment of the vector. Since the segment of the vector owned by a processor exactly matches what the processor accesses, each task is completely local and thus can be implemented efficiently.

Finally, implementation annotations must be added to the declarations of shared data, in this case the three vectors result, a, and b. The type Vector specified for those variables is an abstract data type; a concrete implementation of that data type that supports the mapping **block** is needed. Since this is a common mapping, Par's library contains such a concrete data type named **BlockVector**. Thus, the final version of the program is as follows:

```
program add
    n : 100
    a, b, result : Vector⟨Real⟩(1, n) {use BlockVector}
    {map a, b, result : block}
    co i := 1 to n {scheduler block} →
        result[i] := a[i] + b[i]
    oc
end add
```

Note that the original statement of the algorithm has not been modified. The program can be understood by ignoring the annotations. Assuming that the implementation of the scheduler and the mappings is correct, the program is correct. Moreover, the scheduler and mappings can easily be modified to fit a different architecture without changing the original algorithm.

1.4   Summary

This book presents a method of writing parallel programs that are clear, efficient, and portable. The method begins with a clear statement of the algorithm and adds annotations to create an efficient program. We have designed the Par language to support this method of programming. Besides supporting scheduling and mapping annotations, Par provides good support for modularity and code reuse.

The use of annotations to achieve efficiency allows Par programs to be written in a highly architecture-independent way while still allowing complete control over details of the calculation when necessary. Programs can be tested for correctness before annotations are added since annotations are not required for correctness. The use of annotations also allows programs to be tailored to various architectures without changing the basic (unannotated) program. This allows various strategies for scheduling and mapping to be tried without affecting the correctness of a program.

Using annotations makes it possible to express the original algorithm in a very natural way and still achieve good efficiency. In particular, Par's schedulers allow small chores to be combined into larger tasks at compile time. Except for para-functional programming (see Section 6.9.2), we are aware of no other approach that supports this. Other approaches require that the program be written from the start with a particular granularity in mind.

Par's annotations are written in Par. Other approaches that use annotations either provide only built-in annotations or provide a restricted language in which to implement annotations. Since writing a scheduler or mapping is essentially an exercise in distributed programming, we feel that a good distributed programming language should be available for that purpose. Par's facilities for distributed programming are based on those in SR [10, 11], a highly flexible distributed programming language.

Par provides good support for code reuse. We feel that schedulers and mappings are good candidates for code reuse since they are often specialized implementations of standard data types such as vectors, matrices, and tables.

1.5 Overview

The rest of this book explains our approach to architecture-independent parallel programming in more detail and contrasts it with other approaches. Chapter 2 contains an introduction to the Par language. The purpose is to familiarize the reader with enough of Par so that the rest of the book is understandable.

Chapters 3 and 4 present many examples of the use of our method of writing parallel programs. Chapter 3 explores programming regular algorithms, which have memory-access patterns and chore sizes that do not depend on the input data and can thus be anticipated when the program is written. Chapter 4 explores programming irregular algorithms, whose access patterns and chore sizes cannot be predicted in advance.

Chapter 5 discusses the implementation of Par on various kinds of MIMD computers. Chapter 6 compares and contrasts our approach to architecture-independent parallel programming with alternative methods. Finally, Chapter 7 presents conclusions and ideas for future research.

Chapter 2
The Par Programming Language

Par is a programming language that is designed to explicate the programming method outlined in Chapter 1. It is an explicitly parallel language with provisions for scheduling, mapping, and implementation annotations. It also contains the low-level features necessary to implement annotations efficiently. We chose to design a new language, rather than adapt an existing one, because we wanted to present our programming method in as clear a way a possible; no existing language had the right combination of features for this purpose. However, many of the ideas presented here could be adapted to existing languages. (This is discussed briefly in Chapter 7.)

This chapter provides only a brief overview of the Par language, concentrating on the novel features of the language. Chapters 3 and 4 contain many examples of Par programs.

Par owes a large part of its syntax to SR [10, 11], which is a language for distributed programming. However, Par is quite different from SR; it is not "SR++."

Par is an object-oriented language. The idea of separating the specification of an abstract data type from its implementation is essential to our approach to parallel programming. So too is the idea of extending a type by adding additional operations. Both these concepts fit naturally into an object-oriented language. Many languages have influenced the object-oriented structure of Par. The most important have been Emerald [64], T [107, 93], C++ [110], and Eiffel [87]. The design of the concurrent statement, which specifies parallel execution, owes much to various parallel dialects of FORTRAN, in particular the Force [66].

2.1 Sequential Programming

A Par program consists of statements, declarations, procedures, and processes. Figure 2.1 contains a simple, sequential Par program. Given an integer n_0, this program generates a sequence $n_1, n_2, \ldots$ by the following rule:

$$n_{k+1} = \begin{cases} n_k/2 & \text{if } n_k \text{ is even} \\ 3n_k + 1 & \text{if } n_k \text{ is odd} \end{cases} \tag{2.1}$$

The program stops if $n_k = 1$ and prints the value of k. (If $n_k = 1$ the rest of the sequence is uninteresting—it consists of repetitions of the cycle 4, 2, 1. Whether every initial value for n eventually results in this cycle is unknown.)

```
program does_it_stop
    io : Stdio
    io.print("Number? ");
    n : Int; io.read(n)
    if  n < 0 →   n := −n fi
    k : Int := 0
    do n = 1 → exit
    []  n mod 2 = 0 →  n := n/2; k++
    []  else →  n := 3 * n + 1; k++
    od
    io.print("Terminated after ", k, "iterations\n")
end
```

Figure 2.1: A simple, sequential program.

The first line of the program creates an object named io, which is an instance of the resource Stdio. (We follow the convention that resource names are always capitalized.) Resources are the main unit of encapsulation in Par; they are discussed further in Section 2.5. The resource Stdio exports, among other things, read and print operations that can be used to access the standard input and output streams. After io has been created, the program prints the prompt "Number?," creates an integer n, and reads a value for it. If the value of n is less than zero its sign is reversed; this is accomplished by an alternation (**if**) statement. Then the integer k is declared and set to zero. Finally, the terms of the sequence described in Equation 2.1 are computed until 1 is reached and the final value of k is printed.

Both the alternation (**if ... fi**) and iteration (**do ... od**) statements are built from guarded commands [43, 57], which have the form

guard → block

A *guard* is a boolean expression and a *block* is a sequence of statements and declarations. Boxes ([]) are used to separate guarded commands.

An alternation statement is executed by choosing any true guard and executing the associated block of code. If no guard is true—in the example of Figure 2.1, if $n \geq 0$—the alternation statement terminates with no effect.

An iteration statement is executed by repeatedly choosing any true guard and executing the associated block until either no guard is true or an exit statement is executed. The iteration statment of Figure 2.1 has three guards: $n = 1$, n mod $2 = 0$, and the special guard **else**. The **else** guard is an abbreviation for the negation of the disjunction of the other guards; in this case **else** stands for

$$\neg(n = 1 \lor n \bmod 2 = 0).$$

Thus the iteration statement terminates only when the **exit** statement, corresponding to the guard $n = 1$, is executed.

Although the iteration statement is the only loop construct that is really needed, a more suggestive notation, the for-all statement, is provided for looping over arithmetic progressions. A for-all statement has the following form:

> **fa** id := start **to** finish **by** step $\rightarrow$ block **af**

This statement is equivalent to the following:

```
begin
    id : Int := start
    do id ≤ finish →
        block
        id + := step
    od
end
```

The compound statement (**begin** ... **end**) is needed to ensure that the declaration of id does not interfere with any other visible declarations.

The clause

> id := start **to** finish **by** step

is called the *quantifier* and the identifier id is called the quantifier variable. Quantifier variables are always integers. If "**by** step" is omitted, step defaults to 1. If the direction is **downto** instead of **to**, the sense of the comparison is reversed and the quantifier variable is decremented instead of incremented.

The quantifier variable of a for-all statement can be modified in the body of the statement, although this is not recommended. A quantifier variable is not defined outside its for-all statement; if the value of a quantifier variable is needed outside the for-all statement, it must be assigned to another variable before the statement terminates.

Multiple quantifiers in a for-all statement indicate loop nesting. For example,

> **fa** quant1, quant2 $\rightarrow$ block **af**

is equivalent to

```
fa quant1 →
    fa quant2 → block af
af
```

This extends to any number of quantifiers.

2.2   Declarations and Types

Par is a strongly typed language. Every object has a type and objects must be declared before they are used. Variable declarations have the general form

> name_1, ..., name_n : Type

which creates n instances of Type with the given names. The scope of a declaration extends from the point of declaration to the end of the block in which it occurs. A declaration is visible throughout its scope except where it is masked by a nested declaration with the same name.

Constant declarations have the form

> name : expression

The effect is that name refers to the value of expression. The value of a constant cannot be changed by assignment or by any other operation.

A series of integer constant declarations

> name1 : 1
> name2 : 2
> ...
> nameN : N

can be abbreviated

> enum(name1, name2, ...nameN)

Par's type system is designed to provide both low-level control and high-level support for encapsulation, extensibility, and code reuse. There are several kinds of objects in Par: representations, records, resource instances, references, and operations.

The following sections describe each of these in turn.

2.3   Representations

Processors provide hardware support for certain data types in the form of operations that act on those data types. For example, most processors provide support for 8-bit characters and 32-bit integers. In Par, these hardware-based data types are called *representations*. Every Par implementation provides the following representations:

- Bool_rep is a single bit,

- Char_rep is the standard eight-bit ASCII character type,

- Int_rep is the integer type,

- Real_rep is the floating-point type, and

- Double_rep is the double-precision floating-point type.

An implementation may provide additional representations.

Par also provides built-in functions that operate on representations. These functions are low-level operations that are provided by the processor hardware; they generally require only a few assembly-language instructions to perform. For example, the built-in function int_rep_sum takes as parameters two Int_rep objects and returns their sum.

Representations and built-in functions are rarely needed in user-level code because Par provides standard resources such as Int and Bool that are more convenient to use and just as efficient. These standard resources are implemented in terms of representations and built-in functions.

2.4 Records

Par records are similar to those in other programming languages. For example,

```
record Employee
    name : String
    age : Int
end
```

creates a type Employee with two fields. The fields of a record are accessed using the notation object.field. For example,

```
boss : Employee
boss.name := "Doe, Jane"
boss.age := 35
```

Record literals are also supported. For example, the expression

```
Employee("Doe, Jane", 35)
```

has as its value a record identical to boss above.

Record assignment is allowed between two instances of the same record type. It has the same effect as assigning each field separately. For example, if new_boss is an instance of Employee,

boss := new_boss

has the same effect as

```
boss.name := new_boss.name
boss.age := new_boss.age
```

2.5   Resources

The main unit of encapsulation in Par is the resource. A resource consists of a specification and an optional body. The specification contains declarations of exported objects; everything that is not exported is private to the body of the resource.

Figure 2.2 contains a simple resource that implements a stack of integers. The specification of IntStack declares two operations, push and pop, which form the interface between IntStack and its clients. The internal representation of an IntStack, as well as how the exported operations are implemented, is hidden from the outside world. The internal representation of IntStack consists of three objects: size is a constant with value 100, data is a vector of integers, and ptr is an integer which points to the next free stack location, and hence is initialized to 1. The operations push and pop are implemented by procedures.

Instances of resources are usually created by declarations. For example, a program that uses IntStack is shown in Figure 2.3. Program reverse reads a list of numbers and prints them in reverse order. It accomplishes this by pushing numbers on a stack until io.read returns false—which means that an end-of-file has been reached—and then printing them in reverse order as it pops them from the stack.

There is no need to import resources; the compiler finds them automatically. The user can control how resources are found, but this mechanism is not part of the language. Since even simple objects like integers and boolean values are instances of resources, it would be inconvenient to have to import every resource that is used explicitly.

```
resource IntStack
    op push(Int)
    op pop() returns Int
body
    size : 100
    data : Vector⟨Int⟩(1, size)
    ptr : Int := 1
    proc push(item : Int)
        if  ptr > size → abort("stack full")
        []  else → data[ptr] := item; ptr++
        fi
    end
    proc pop()
        if  ptr = 1 → abort("stack empty")
        []  else → ptr − −; return data[ptr]
        fi
    end
end IntStack
```

Figure 2.2: A stack of integers

```
# reverse the input numbers
program reverse
    io : Stdio
    istk : IntStack
    count : Int := 0
    i : Int;
    do io.read(i) →
        istk.push(i); count++
    od
    do count > 0 →
        io.print(istk.pop()); count − −
    od
end
```

Figure 2.3: Using IntStack.

2.5.1   Initial and Final.

A resource can specify one or more initial operations. The initial operations must differ in number or type of formal parameters. When an instance of the resource is created, actual parameters to one of the initial operations are specified; the initial operation whose formal parameter specification matches the actual initial parameters is invoked. An initial operation can perform arbitrary computation but it usually is used to allocate space, initialize variables, or set up communication channels to other objects.

Figure 2.4 contains code for a stack resource that allows programs that use the resource to specify a maximum stack size.   This resource has several interesting features. The object size is a variable that is initialized to 100 instead of a constant as it was in the previous version. The first (parameterless) initial operation allows a stack to be created without specifying a size; in that case the size defaults to 100, the same value as in the previous implementation. The second initial operation allows the user to specify a maximum size when an instance of IntStack is declared, as in

```
short_stack : IntStack(10)
big_stack : IntStack(10000)
```

When an instance of IntStack is created, one of the initial operations allocates space for data dynamically with a *naming statement*:

$$\text{data} \leftarrow \text{Vector}\langle\text{Int}\rangle(1, \text{size})$$

The expression on the right-hand side of the arrow creates an anonymous instance of Vector that has an indefinite lifetime. The object data, which is declared to be a reference to a vector of integers, becomes a name for the anonymous vector. References and naming statements are discussed in more detail in Section 2.6.

A resource can contain a single final block, which is executed when the object is destroyed. Final blocks are generally used to de-allocate storage, close communication channels, or perform other cleanup. In Figure 2.4, the final block de-allocates the object referred to by data.

2.5.2   Generic Resources

Resources can be *generic*. A generic resource is parameterized by one or more types. The actual types are specified when an instance of the resource is created. The resource Vector, used in both Figure 2.2 and Figure 2.4, is a generic resource; the generic parameter specifies the base type of the vector.

Figure 2.5 contains an implementation of a generic stack.   The reader should find this familiar since almost the only changes that have been made from Figure 2.4

```
resource IntStack
    op push(Int)
    op pop() returns Int
    op initial()
    op initial(maxsize : Int)
body
    data : ref⟨Vector⟨Int⟩⟩
    ptr : Int := 1
    size : Int := 100
    proc initial()
        data ← Vector⟨Int⟩(1, size)
    end
    proc initial(d : Int)
        size := d
        data ← Vector⟨Int⟩(1, size)
    end
    proc push(item : Int)
        if  ptr > size →  abort("stack full")
        []  else →  data[ptr] := item; ptr++
        fi
    end
    proc pop()
        if  ptr = 1 →  abort("stack empty")
        []  else →  ptr − −; return data[ptr]
        fi
    end
    final
        destroy(data)
    end
end IntStack
```

Figure 2.4: A variable-sized stack of integers.

```
resource Stack⟨T⟩
    op push(T)
    op pop() returns T
    op initial()
    op initial(maxsize : Int)
body
    data : ref⟨Vector⟨T⟩⟩
    ptr : Int := 1
    size : Int := 100
    proc initial()
        data ← Vector⟨T⟩(1, size)
    end
    proc initial(d : Int)
        size := d
        data ← Vector⟨T⟩(1, size)
    end
    proc push(item : T)
        if  ptr > size →  abort("stack full")
        []  else →  data[ptr] := item; ptr++
        fi
    end
    proc pop()
        if  ptr = 1 →  abort("stack empty")
        []  else →  ptr − −; return data[ptr]
        fi
    end
    final
        destroy(data)
    end
end Stack
```

Figure 2.5: A generic stack

are that most uses of Int have been changed to the generic parameter T. The generic resource Stack can be used as a template for stacks of various types. For example,

```
int_stk : Stack⟨Int⟩
real_stk : Stack⟨Real⟩
```

creates two stacks—one of integers, the other of real numbers.

An actual generic parameter must export any operations that are applied to objects of the generic type in the body of the resource. In Figure 2.5, for example, the assign operation is applied to objects of type T; thus any actual type specified for T must export an assign operation. (Both Int and Real do so.) The compiler checks this condition. This approach is similar to that taken in the proposed addition of generic classes to C++ [110] in that the compiler is responsible for determining which actual generic parameters are legal. It differs from languages such as Eiffel [87] that require the programmer to specify which operations must be exported by generic formals. It also differs from languages such as Ada [9] and Orca [15], which require that all operations applied to objects of a generic type must be additional parameters to the generic module.

2.5.3 Subtypes

A resource R is a *subtype* of resource S—and S is a *supertype* of R—if R exports all the operations exported by S and perhaps others. For example, suppose that Polygon has the specification

```
resource Polygon
    op edge_list() returns Edgelist
    op area() returns Real
end
```

and that Square has the specification

```
resource Square
    op edge_list() returns Edgelist
    op area() returns Real
    op diagonal() returns Real
end
```

Then **Square** is a subtype of **Polygon** because it exports all the operations of **Polygon**. Any type-correct use of a **Polygon** is also a type-correct use of a **Square**.

When defining a subtype of another type, it can be inconvenient to repeat the entire specification of the supertype; thus Par provides an **extends** declaration, which has exactly the same effect. For example, a terser way to write the specification of **Square** is

> **resource** Square
>   **extends** Polygon
>   **op** diagonal() **returns** Real
> **end**

Besides shortening the specification of **Square**, the extends declaration makes the subtype-supertype relationship between Polygon and Square more obvious.

2.5.4   Standard Resources

Par provides standard resources for the usual types: **Bool, Char, Int, Real, String,** etc. Each standard resource exports operations that perform initialization, assignment, and other (type-specific) operations. The implementation of standard resources is not specified.

A processor is not object-oriented; it operates only on hardware representations. Thus a way is needed to obtain a representation from a resource. For example, a processor does not manipulate objects of type **Int**; the hardware is designed for objects of type **Int_rep**. Thus each of the standard resources exports an operation **rep** that takes no parameters and returns a hardware representation of the object. Generally, the representation is used only to define higher level operations on the resource.

For example, the resource **Int** exports the following operation:

> **op** rep() **returns** Int_rep

This allows operations on objects of type **Int** to be defined in terms of operations on **Int_rep**. For example, the sum of two instances of **Int, a** and **b**, could be expressed as

> Int(int_rep_sum(a.rep(), b.rep()))

Recall that int_rep_sum is a built-in function that adds two objects of type **Int_rep**. Thus the expression above extracts the representations of **a** and **b**, adds them, and constructs a new instance of **Int** using the sum as the initial parameter.

2.6 References

A *reference* is an object that refers to (names) another object. A reference declaration specifies the name of the reference and the type of object to which it will refer. For example,

r : **ref**⟨Vector⟨Int⟩⟩

declares r to be a reference to a vector of integers.

A reference is affixed to an existing object by a naming statement. For example, if v is a vector of integers, the naming statement

r ← v

causes r to refer to v. Thereafter, r is an alias for v (with a few exceptions enumerated below). Thus if the statment

r[3] := 9

is executed, the expressions $v[3]$ and $r[3]$ will both yield 9.

A reference can refer to any object whose type is a subtype of the reference type. For example, if Square is a subtype of Polygon (as in Section 2.5.3) the following fragment is legal:

p : **ref**⟨Polygon⟩
sq : Square
p ← sq

However, since Par is statically typed, p must be treated as a name for a Polygon even though it refers (temporarily, perhaps) to a Square. For example,

p.diagonal()

is illegal because diagonal is not exported by Polygon.

Naming statements are often used in conjunction with dynamic allocation. For example, in the resource IntStack of Section 2.5 (Figure 2.2), the variable data is declared to be a reference to a vector of integers:

data : **ref**⟨Vector⟨Int⟩⟩

The actual vector is allocated dynamically and data becomes a name for it:

```
resource List⟨T⟩
    op initial()
    op to_left()
    op right() returns Bool
    op put(T)
    op remove()
    op value() returns T
    op empty() returns Bool
end
```

Figure 2.6: Specification for List

---

data ← Vector⟨Int⟩(1, size)

The expression on the right-hand side of the arrow creates an anonymous vector of integers. (In general, type descriptors can be used either to declare types or as allocators.) The name data is immediately affixed to this object.

A few special operations are allowed on references. The reference comparison operators == and ! == compare two references to determine whether they refer to the same object; for example,

```
if  r1 == r2 → io.print("r1 and r2 are the same")
[] r1! == r2 → io.print("r1 and r2 are different")
fi
```

The built-in function null returns true if and only if the reference to which it is applied does not refer to any object.

A reference is an alias for the object to which it refers except when it used in one of the following ways:

- on the left-hand side of a naming statement,

- as an operand of == or ! ==,

- as the operand of the built-in function null.

As a practical example of the use of references, we give the implementation of a generic List resource. Figure 2.6 contains the specification of List. This resource provides a cursor-based model of a list. In this model, a list consists of a sequence of items (aligned from left to right) and a cursor. A list initially consists of an anchor, which is a dummy item that has no value. The cursor can be "on" any item in the list; it is originally on the anchor. The user can move the cursor one element to the right

```
body
    record Node
        value : T
        next : ref⟨Node⟨T⟩⟩
        prev : ref⟨Node⟨T⟩⟩
    end
    anchor, cursor : ref⟨Node⟨T⟩⟩
    proc initial()
        anchor ← Node
        cursor ← anchor
    end
    ...
end
```

Figure 2.7: Internal representation of List

by invoking right, or to its original position by invoking to_left. The value of the item under the cursor is returned by value. The remove operation removes the item under the cursor from the list and leaves the cursor pointing to the previous item. (It is illegal to invoke value or remove if the cursor is on the anchor.) The put operation inserts a new item to the right of the current item; it does not move the cursor. The empty operation returns true if the list is empty.

Figure 2.7 contains the declarations of the internal representation of List, along with the initial procedure. Internally, a List is represented by a doubly-linked chain of objects of type Node. A node has three fields, value, next, and prev. The value field contains the value of the list element, the next field contains a reference to the next list element, and the prev field contains a reference to the previous list element. The initial operation creates the anchors and sets cursor to point to the anchor.

Figure 2.8 contains code for the cursor-movement operations. The procedure to_left moves the cursor to its original position by setting cursor to anchor. The procedure right returns false if the cursor is on the right-most item, otherwise it moves the cursor to the next item and returns true. Thus the standard way to iterate through all elements of a List is as follows:

```
lst.to_left()
do lst.right() →
    # use "lst.value"
od
```

```
# move cursor to left end
proc to_left()
    cursor ← anchor
end
# move cursor one right if possible
proc right()
    if  null(cursor.next) →  return false
    []  prev ← cursor; cursor ← cursor.next
    fi
end
```

Figure 2.8: Cursor movement operations

Figure 2.9 contains the operations used to insert and remove items from the list. Procedure insert creates a new Node, sets the value field to the proper value, and links the node into the list. Procedure remove first checks to ensure that cursor does not refer to anchor; then it removes the node referred to by cursor.

Finally, Figure 2.10 contains the empty and value procedures and the final block. The empty procedure uses the built-in function null to determine whether the reference anchor.next refers to an object. The value procedure simply returns the value field of the node under the cursor if that node is not the anchor. The final block iterates through the list, de-allocating each node.

2.7   Operations

2.7.1   Invoking Operations

Resources communicate by invoking and servicing operations. Operation invocation has already been seen several times. The most obvious kinds of invocations are expressions of the form

```
operation(argument, ...)
```

or

```
object.operation(argument, ...)
```

For example,

```
foo(3.0)
```

```
# insert item after cursor
proc insert(item : T)
    temp : ref⟨Node⟩ ← Node
    temp.value := item
    temp.next ← cursor.next
    cursor.next ← temp
end
# remove cursor item
proc remove()
    if  cursor == anchor →
        abort("Illegal list operation: remove anchor")
    []  else →
        temp : ref⟨Node⟩ ← cursor
        cursor ← cursor.prev
        cursor.next ← cursor.next.next
        destroy(temp)
    fi
end
```

Figure 2.9: List modification procedures

invokes the operation foo, which must be declared in the current program or resource, while

stk.push(item)

invokes the push operation exported by the object stk.

However, invocation is even more prevalent than it might appear because Par's expression syntax is just disguised invocation. For example, the stack pointer in each of Figures 2.2, 2.4, and 2.5 was incremented by writing

ptr++

which is just shorthand for

ptr.post_increment()

Similarly, ptr was initialized by writing

ptr := 0

which is shorthand for

```
proc empty()
    return null(anchor.next)
end
proc value()
    if  cursor == anchor →
        abort("Illegal list operation: value of anchor")
    []  else →
        return cursor.value
    fi
end
final
    t1, t2 : ref⟨Node⟩
    t1 ← anchor
    do  not null(t1) →
        t2 ← t1
        t1 ← t1.next
        destroy(t2)
    od
end
```

Figure 2.10: The empty procedure and the final block

---

ptr.assign(0)

In Par, all expressions are just disguised invocations.

Operation invocation can be synchronous or asynchronous. Synchronous invocation is the default. A synchronous invocation delays the invoking process until the invocation completes. Synchronous invocations can return results. Asynchronous invocations are specified by send statements; for example:

send stk.push(3)

Asynchronous invocation does not delay the invoker; instead both the invoking and the invoked operations proceed concurrently. If an operation that returns a result is invoked asynchronously, the result is discarded.

Invocations can be performed locally or remotely. By default, operations that are serviced by procedures (Section 2.7.2) are executed on the invoker's processor, and operations that are serviced by input statements (Section 2.7.2) are executed on the processor on which the operation resides. The default can be overridden by an **on** clause; for example,

> foo(3, 4) **on** 7
> **send** bar() **on** 7

This has the effect of invoking both foo and bar on processor 7.

Par has two parameter passing mechanisms, depending on whether the type of the formal parameter is a resource type or a reference type. Resource parameters provide call-by-value semantics; reference parameters provide call-by-reference semantics.

If a formal parameter has a resource type, the formal parameter names a new object, which is obtained by creating an instance of the resource. The actual parameter is used as the initial parameter in the creation. For example, consider the following operation declaration:

> **op** boo(k : Int)

If the invocation

> boo(7)

is executed, the integer k is created with initial parameter 7. It is much as if the declaration

> k : Int(7)

were shared between the invoker and the body of the operation. The invoker supplies the initial parameter and the body of the operation uses it to create k.

If the resource specified by a formal parameter exports several initial operations, the actual parameter can match any one of them. For example, the resource Real provides the following initial operations:

> **op** initial(Real)
> **op** initial(Int)

An operation that specifies a formal parameter of type Real can accept an actual parameter that matches either of these operations. For example, if sin is declared as

> **op** sin(r : Real) **returns** Real

then the invocations

> sin(3)
> sin(3.4)

are both legal. In the first invocation, the formal parameter is created with 3 as the initial parameter, which has the effect of coercing 3 to a real number. It is as if the declaration

> r : Real(3)

were shared between the invoker and the body of sin.

When a formal parameter is a reference type, the formal parameter becomes an alias for the object that results when the actual parameter is evaluated. Reference parameters are specified by using a reference type in the formal parameter specification; for example,

> **op** boo(k : **ref**⟨Int⟩)... **end**

When boo is serviced, k will refer to the object that is used as the actual parameter. For example, if boo is invoked as

> boo(x)

it is as if the declaration

> k : **ref**⟨Int⟩ ← x

were shared between the invoker and the operation. With call by reference, the actual parameter must be a subtype of the formal type.

Operations can have optional parameters that are specified by name. For example, the following declaration specifies two mandatory parameters and two optional parameters:

> **op** foo(a, b : Real, **optional** c : Int(0), d : Int(3))

If foo is invoked by

> foo(3.4, 4.5)

then c and d default to 0 and 3, respectively. Non-default values are specified in the following way:

> foo(3.4, 4.5, d := 12, c := 17)

Optional parameters can appear in any order, but they must appear after the required parameters.

An operation can return more than one result. For example,

return(x, y)

returns both x and y. Multiple return values must be enclosed in parenthesis. An operation that returns multiple results can be used only in the context of an assignment statement that has multiple target variables. For example, if the operation sin_cos returns two real numbers, it could be used in the following way:

s, c := sin_cos(x)

The effect is that s receives the first value returned and c the second.

2.7.2 Servicing Operations

Procedures

An operation can be serviced either by a procedure or by one or more input statements. Some examples of procedures—e.g., push and pop in Figures 2.2, 2.4, and 2.5— have already been presented. A procedure is a template for the implementation of an operation. When an operation is implemented by a procedure, each invocation conceptually creates a new process to service the invocation and transmits the actual parameters to the new process. (Often, however, such invocations can be compiled into standard procedure calls.) If the invocation is asynchronous, the invoker and the instance of the procedure execute concurrently. If the invocation is synchronous, the invoker waits for the process to terminate. When the invoked procedure terminates, the result is transmitted back to the invoker.

A procedure name can be either the name of a previously declared operation or the name of a resource. If a procedure name is the name of an operation, the procedure implements that operation. If the procedure name is the name of a resource, the procedure is a template for the implementation of all the operations exported by that resource. Since the arguments of the invocation are not available to such a procedure, it can accomplish only a limited amount on its own. However, the procedure can *delegate* the invocation to another object. For example, Figure 2.11 contains an implementation of Square, which adds a diagonal operation to Polygon. The diagonal operation is implemented in Square, while the rest of the operations are delegated to an instance of Polygon. Note that the resource Square never explicitly names the operations of Polygon; thus Polygon could be modified without modifying Square.

Par uses delegation rather than inheritance to provide code reuse. In this it follows the example of such languages as T [93] and Act 1 [79], and breaks with most other object-oriented languages. Delegation separates the ideas of specification reuse and code reuse, while inheritance combines them. We feel that code reuse is an (important) implementation detail that should not affect the specification of an object. For a comparison of inheritance and delegation see [80].

```
resource Square
    extends Polygon
    op diagonal() returns Real
body
    local_poly : Polygon
    proc Polygon
        delegate local_poly
    end
    proc diagonal()
        # body
    end
end
```

Figure 2.11: Resource Square extends Polygon.

```
in  push(item : T) →
    if  ptr > size → abort("stack full")
    []  else → data[ptr] := item; ptr++
    fi
[]  pop() →
    if  ptr ≤ 1 → abort("stack empty")
    []  else → ptr − −; return data[ptr]
    fi
ni
```

Figure 2.12: An input statement

Input statements.

The second way to service invocations is by input statements. Figure 2.12 is an example of an input statement that services the operations push and pop: A process that executes this statement is delayed until an invocation of push or pop is available; then the appropriate block of code is executed and the process continues. This input statement could be substituted for the two procedures push and pop in Figure 2.5. Like a procedure, an input statement can name a set of operations by using a resource name instead of an operation name.

An input statement can service invocations selectively. In the previous implementations of stacks, an overflow or underflow aborted the computation. Another possibility is to delay servicing operations until they are guaranteed to complete. This can be done using *synchronization expressions*. For example:

```
in  push(item : T) and ptr ≤ size →
    data[ptr] := item; ptr++
[]  pop() and ptr > 1 →
    ptr − −; return data[ptr]
ni
```

Now the process that executes the input statement delays either until an invocation of push is available and the stack is not full or until an invocation of pop is available and the stack is not empty.

A synchronization expression can depend on the formal parameters of the operation being serviced. For example, a vector of semaphores can be implemented as follows:

```
count : Vector⟨Int⟩(1, n)
fa  i := 1 to n →  count[i] := 0 af
do true →
    in  p(i : Int) and count[i] > 0 →  count − −;
    []  v(i : Int) →  count[i]++
    ni
od
```

The vector count is initialized to zeros. The semaphore server loops forever, servicing invocations of p and v. Since they are serviced by the same process, invocations are serviced one at a time. The synchronization expression delays service to a p operation until the appropriate element of count is positive.

Processes.   In low-level programming, it is often convenient for an object to contain processes that start when the resource is created and terminate only when the resource is destroyed. For example, a common pattern is to enclose an input statement in an infinite loop inside such a process. This is easy to accomplish using asynchronous invocation of procedures, but the pattern is so common that a special **process** construct is provided.

For example, Figure 2.13 contains code for a resource that implements a semaphore. The process specification accomplishes three things: it implicitly declares an operation sem_server, it declares a procedure to implement the operation, and it arranges that the operation be automatically invoked when an instance of the resource is created.

Several instances of a process can be specified by appending a quantifier to the process heading; for example,

```
resource Semaphore
   op p()
   op v()
body
   process sem_server
      count : Int := 0
      do true →
         in p() and count > 0 →  count − −;
         [] v() →  count++
         ni
      od
   end
end Semaphore
```

Figure 2.13: A Semaphore resource

---

process zed(i := 1 **to** 10)... **end**

creates 10 instances of the process zed. Each receives a different value of i as a parameter.

2.8   Concurrency

The main way to get parallel execution in Par is the concurrent (**co** ... **oc**) statement.
A concurrent statement is syntactically similar to a for-all statement. For example, a
sequential loop to add two vectors might be written as

fa i := 1 **to** n → a[i] := b[i] + c[i] **af**

while a concurrent statement for the same purpose would be written

co i := 1 **to** n → a[i] := b[i] + c[i] **oc**

The difference is that in the for-all statement the individual additions must be executed
sequentially, while in the concurrent statement they can be executed concurrently.

Each instance of the body of a concurrent statement is called a *chore*. Above, there
are n chores:

a[i] := b[i] + c[i]

for i in 1...n. Chores represent the natural units of parallelism exhibited by an algorithm. (However, chores are not atomic units of parallelism; concurrent statements
can be nested, so chores can contain sub-chores.) The way that chores are combined
into tasks and assigned to processors is specified by scheduling annotations, which are
discussed in Section 2.10.2. In the example above, all the chores access the vectors
a, b, and c. Par supports a shared name space and thus allows a shared-memory style
of programming. However, Par does not attempt to simulate *uniform access* shared
memory. Instead, mapping annotations allow the programmer to control the placement
of objects. Mapping annotations are discussed in Section 2.10.3.

A concurrent statement can have multiple arms, each with its own quantifier. For
example, the concurrent statement

```
co i := 1 to n →  a[i] := b[i] + c[i] -
//  j := 1 to n →  d[i] := b[i] * c[i]
//    →  x := y + z
oc
```

has three arms. The first specifies n chores, each of which consists of an addition and
an assignment. The second also specifies n chores, each of which is a multiplication
and an assignment. The third specifies a single chore. All these chores are executed
in parallel.

Chores can contain *barriers*. A barrier is a synchronization point; all the chores
must reach a barrier before any can proceed past it. For example,

```
co i := 1 to n →
    # add two vectors
    c[i] := a[i] + b[i]
    barrier
    # smooth the result
    c[i] := c[i − 1] + 2 * c[i] + c[i + 1]
oc
```

In this example, it is important that the elements of c are computed before they are
used; thus a barrier is placed between the definition and the use.

In general, concurrent statements with barriers can be rewritten with multiple concurrent statements. The example above could have been written as follows:

```
co i := 1 to n →
    # add two vectors
    c[i] := a[i] + b[i]
oc
co i := 1 to n →
    # smooth the result
    c[i] := c[i − 1] + 2 ∗ c[i] + c[i + 1]
oc
```

Using a barrier obviates the need to repeat the quantifier.

2.9   Distributed Data Structures

Par supports the implementation of distributed data structures; the built-in resource IdVector is the basis for building them. The specification of IdVector is as follows:

```
resource IdVector⟨T⟩
    extends Vector⟨T⟩
    op initial()
end
```

An IdVector is a vector that is implemented so that each element of the vector resides on a different physical processor. The parameterless initial operation creates a vector with one vector element for each processor. Figure 2.14 shows the effect of the following code fragment, assuming a 4-processor multicomputer with processors numbered $0 \ldots 3$.

```
a : IdVector⟨Real⟩
b : IdVector⟨ref⟨Vector⟨Real⟩⟩⟩(1, 3)
```

Since a has no initial parameters, the range defaults to $0 \ldots 3$. The object b is an IdVector (with range $1 \ldots 3$) of references to real-valued vectors. Thus b[1] is stored on processor 1, b[2] on processor 2, and b[3] on processor 3.

As a simple illustration of the use of IdVector, we define a generic resource called Private, which keeps, on each processor, an independent copy of an object.   For example, the declaration

```
a : Private⟨Int⟩
```

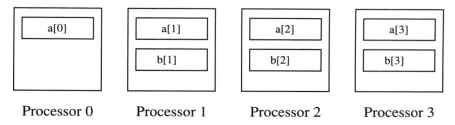

Figure 2.14: The physical layout of IdVector resources.

```
resource Private⟨T⟩
    extends T
body
    rep : IdVector⟨T⟩
    proc T
        delegate rep[@]
    end
end
```

Figure 2.15: The generic resource Private

will result in num_procs different integers, one per processor. Each access to a is made to the local integer; thus the value of a can depend on which processor uses it.

Figure 2.15 contains the definition of Private. The internal representation of a Private object is an IdVector. The procedure T delegates all operations exported by the generic type T to the local element of the IdVector. The notation "@" is an abbreviation for cur_proc, the current processor number.

For example, suppose that stk is declared as

stk : Private⟨Stack⟨Int⟩⟩

Then if processor 3 executes the invocation

stk.push(7)

then the push operation will be delegated to rep[3], which, since rep is an IdVector, is an instance of Stack that resides on processor 3. If the same invocation were executed by processor 4, push(7) would be delegated to rep[4], an instance of Stack on processor 4. The effect is that each processor has a private stack of integers; hence the name Private.

Chapters 3 and 4 contain many more examples of distributed data structures.

2.10   Annotations

Par programs are *annotated* to tailor them to a particular computer or class of computers. Annotations are never required; they affect only efficiency, not correctness. The meaning of a program can be understood by disregarding annotations. To emphasize this, annotations are separated syntactically from the rest of the program by enclosing them in braces.

We first describe the model of computation on which Par annotations are based. Then we describe the annotations themselves and how each is implemented. The use of annotations is the main topic of Chapters 3 and 4 so the description here is brief.

2.10.1   Model of Computation

Par annotations are based on a simple model of MIMD computation. A computer consists of a collection of processors and a collection of memory modules. Each processor is associated with one memory module, which is termed the *local memory* of that processor. Other modules are addressable but nonlocal Access to local memory is at least as fast as access to nonlocal memory.

Processors and memory modules are numbered; a processor and its local memory module have the same number. On any particular computer these numbers are assigned in some systematic way. For example, on a hypercube, the processors would be numbered using the standard Gray-code scheme. Thus annotations designed for a particular computer can use the structure implicit in the numbering scheme to provide efficient interprocessor communication.

During execution, a program can obtain several parameters that describe the current computer. The built-in function num_procs returns the number of processors. Similarly, min_proc and max_proc return the minimum and maximum processor numbers. The function cur_proc, which can be abbreviated "@" ("at"), returns the current processor number.

Par's run-time system provides remote memory access. Any processor can

- allocate space in any memory module,

- store a value at a specified address in any memory module, and

- retrieve the value at a specified address in any memory module.

However, Par makes no attempt to conceal the cost of remote access. On NUMA computers and (especially) on multicomputers, the three operations mentioned above will execute much faster if the specified memory module is local. The implementation of these operations is architecture dependent and is described further in Chapter 5.

A Par program initially consists of a single main thread executing on a single processor. Asynchronous invocation, processes, and concurrent statements cause new threads to be forked. Sequential flow-of-control statements within a thread are executed in the usual way. However, executing a statement may require a thread to access remote values. Remote access is handled automatically but, again, no attempt is made to hide its cost.

Declarations of primitive, machine-defined types are accomplished by allocating space in the memory module local to the current thread. Thus, for example, the declaration

    a : Int

allocates space for an integer on the processor cur_proc. Threads on other processors can access a, but access will be remote, and hence slower. A consequence of the fact that a is accessible from any processor is that each processor must know where a is—that is, in which memory module a resides and at what address in that module. How this is accomplished depends on the architecture and is described further in Chapter 5.

Declarations of IdVector are elaborated in a similar fashion except that the processor performing the elaboration allocates space in each specified memory module instead of only on its own. Again, all processors must know where each element of the IdVector resides.

Declarations of resource types are elaborated by executing the body of the resource and then invoking an initial operation. Unless concurrency is explicitly specified in the body of the resource or in the initial operation, the declaration is elaborated on a single processor. Except for scoping and naming considerations, declaring a resource type is essentially equivalent to substituting the body of the resource at the point of the declaration.

Constants are evaluated once and then replicated on all processors that can access them; thus mapping of constants is not necessary.

Asynchronous invocation is implemented by forking a single light-weight process and passing the specified parameters. The execution of the concurrent statement is described in Section 2.10.2.

2.10.2 Scheduling Annotations

Scheduling is specified in Par by adding *scheduling annotations* to concurrent statements. For example,

    co i := 1 **to** N {**scheduler** block} $\rightarrow$ a[i] := b[i] + c[i] **oc**

specifies that the scheduler named block is responsible for executing the chores named in the concurrent statement. A concurrent statement with more than one arm can have a scheduling annotation added to each arm.

To write schedulers it is important to know something about the way concurrent statements are implemented. When a concurrent statement is executed, the effect is to invoke the scheduler once on each processor of the computer. Thus, many copies of the scheduler are simultaneously invoked. The schedulers, collectively, are responsible for executing each chore exactly once. They can do this by statically dividing the chores among themselves or by cooperating with each other at run time.

A scheduler performs a single chore by executing a **chore** statement. For example, one of the copies of the scheduler segment could execute the chore

$$a[3] := b[3] + c[3]$$

by executing the statement

    chore(3)

Here is a simple example of a scheduler:

```
scheduler odd_even(p, l, u, step : Int)
    fa i := l to u by step →
        if  p = 1 and odd(i) →  chore(i)
        []  p = 2 and even(i) →  chore(i)
        fi
    af
end
```

The first parameter is the processor number on which this instance of the scheduler is executing. Each instance of the scheduler will have a different value for p. The integers l, u, and step are the lower-bound, upper-bound, and step size of the concurrent-statement quantifier. All instances of the scheduler receive the same values for these parameters. This scheduler executes all odd-numbered chores on processor 1 and all even-numbered chores on processor 2. The processors do not need to communicate since the mapping is static.

The set of processors that execute a scheduler can be restricted to a subset of the available processors by the use of an **on** clause in the scheduler annotation. For example,

    {**scheduler** odd_even **on** 1 **to** 10}

executes the odd_even scheduler only on processors 1 . . . 10. The annotation

{**on** 7}

executes all the chores of a concurrent statement on processor 7.

Sometimes it is convenient to curtail parallelism completely in some concurrent statement. For example, a computer with only a few processors may not be able to take advantage of some of the parallelism in a particular algorithm. The built-in scheduler forall has the effect of implementing a concurrent statement as a for-all statement. That is,

$$\textbf{co} \ i := 1 \ \textbf{to} \ n, j := 1 \ \textbf{to} \ n \ \{\textbf{scheduler} \ \text{forall}\} \rightarrow \ ... \ \textbf{oc}$$

is computationally equivalent to

$$\textbf{fa} \ i := 1 \ \textbf{to} \ n, j := 1 \ \textbf{to} \ n \rightarrow \ ... \ \textbf{af}$$

The former statement is clearer because it expresses the fact that the chores could be computed in parallel. Also, if the program is ported to another computer that can take advantage of the parallelism, it will be easy to change the scheduler.

A common use of the concurrent statement is to create one chore on each processor. This could be written

$$\textbf{co} \ p := \text{min\_proc}() \ \textbf{to} \ \text{max\_proc}() \ \{\textbf{scheduler} \ \text{id\_scheduler}\} \rightarrow \ ... \ \textbf{oc}$$

where id_scheduler is a scheduler that executes chore p on processor p. However, this case is so common that the following abbreviation is used:

$$\textbf{co} \ p := \text{processors} \rightarrow \ ...\textbf{oc}$$

The name processors is simply a macro that expands to the following:

$$\text{min\_proc}() \ \textbf{to} \ \text{max\_proc}() \ \{\textbf{scheduler} \ \text{id\_scheduler}\}$$

Ocassionally, it is useful to be able to share objects between various instances of the same scheduler. (For an example, see the implementation of the scheduler fcfs in Section 4.1.1.) This can be accomplished by using the keyword **shared** in the object declaration; for example:

$$\textbf{shared} \ \text{size} : \text{int}$$

All uses of size in instances of the scheduler containing the declaration above will refer to the same integer.

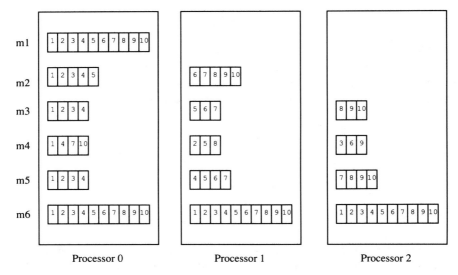

Figure 2.16: Some examples of mapping vectors to processors

2.10.3 Mapping Annotations

Suppose that a vector v is declared as follows:

v : Vector⟨Int⟩(1, 10)

On parallel computers, there are many ways to store such a vector. For example, Figure 2.16 shows several ways that v could be stored on a three-processor parallel computer. Each row represents a possible mapping. Mapping m1 maps all elements of the vector to processor 0; access to the vector is local for processor 0 and nonlocal for processors 1 and 2. Mappings m2, m3, and m4 partition the vector in various ways. Mapping m5 is not a partition since elements 4 and 7 are replicated on two processors. Finally, mapping m6 replicates all elements on all three processors. When a mapping replicates elements, the definition of the mapping must use suitable protocols to ensure that copies of replicated elements remain consistent.

The best mapping for a data structure depends on both the architecture of the parallel computer and the way that the data structure is used. Furthermore, it can be useful to change mappings during the course of a calculation. Specification of a mapping, or change of mapping, is accomplished by the use of mapping annotations. For example,

v : Vector⟨Int⟩(1, 10)
...
{**map** v : m3}

remaps v into the mapping m3.

Mappings are implemented as operations. The annotation above, for example, has the effect of invoking the operation m3 of the object v:

> v.m3()

Thus v must export the operation m3. This is a problem since v is declared to be an instance of Vector, which does not export m3 (or any other mapping). The solution to this problem is the subject of the next section.

2.10.4   Implementation Annotations

An implementation annotation specifies a concrete implementation for an abstract data type. For example, if DistVector is some implementation of a vector, the following annotation could be used:

> v : Vector⟨Int⟩(1, 10) {**use** DistVector}

The effect is that v will be an instance of resource DistVector rather than Vector. The most common use of implementation annotations is to specify a distributed implementation of a data structure suited to a particular computer and algorithm.

The concrete resource that implements an abstract data type can export more operations than the abstract data type. Often, such extra operations implement various mappings of the data structure. For example, the specification of DistVector might be as follows:

> **resource** DistVector⟨T⟩
>   **extends** Vector⟨T⟩
>   **op** m1(), m2(), m3()
> **end**

The operations m1, m2, and m3 could implement the first three mappings shown in Figure 2.16. If v were declared as

> v : Vector⟨Int⟩(1, 10)

then the mapping of v could be changed by using mapping annotations such as

> {**map** v : m2}

Chapters 3 and 4 contain many examples of concrete resources and of the implementation and use of mappings.

Any extra operations that are exported by a concrete resource can only be used in other annotations. This ensures that annotations can be removed without changing the meaning of a program. For example, outside an annotation, the invocation

    v.m1()

would be illegal since the operation m1 is not exported by Vector.

2.10.5   Declaration Annotations

It is occasionally necessary to create new objects for use in other annotations. This can be accomplished by enclosing a declaration in braces; e.g.,

    {a : Int}

The effect is the same as the declaration

    a : Int

except that in the first case a can only be used inside other annotations.

Chapter 3

Regular Problems

This chapter shows how regular algorithms can be programmed in a portable, efficient, and clear way. By a *regular* algorithm we mean an algorithm whose flow of control and patterns of access are relatively independent of the input data and thus are predictable. The predictability of regular algorithms allows the use of static schedulers and mappings, which tend to be simpler and more efficient than dynamic schedulers and mappings.

As stated in Chapter 1, the Par method of writing architecture-independent parallel programs consists of the following steps:

1. Pick a parallel algorithm.

2. Write a program that is a clean, direct statement of the algorithm, without regard for the target architecture. Use abstract data types in declarations. Express concurrency explicitly and in units natural to the algorithm (*chores*).

3. Add scheduling annotations to concurrent statements to cluster chores into tasks (units of parallelism that can be efficiently implemented) and assign tasks to processors.

4. Add mapping annotations to ensure that data references in tasks are (at least mostly) local to the processor to which the task has been assigned.

5. Add implementation annotations to specify concrete resources for abstract data types. The concrete resource must export all the mappings that are applied to the object.

6. If necessary, provide implementations of the concrete data types and schedulers that are used.

The rest of this chapter contains a series of examples illustrating the Par method:

Matrix addition is a simple example of the Par approach.

Trapezoidal integration is another simple example that introduces an efficient way to implement reduction operations.

```
a, b, s : Matrix⟨Real⟩(1, n, 1, n)
# read values for a and b
...
co i := 1 to n, j := 1 to n →
    s[i, j] := a[i, j] + b[i, j]
oc
```

Figure 3.1: The basic matrix addition program

Matrix multiplication introduces *virtual architectures* and shows how replication can be used to reduce access time.

Region labeling combines several features from earlier examples and illustrates the use of remapping.

Gaussian elimination illustrates more interesting and intricate mappings and schedulers.

Sorting gives a general method by which compare-exchange sorting algorithms can be adapted to MIMD computers. The method is illustrated with odd-even transposition sort and Batcher's merge-exchange sort.

Each example is developed using the method outlined above.

3.1   Matrix Addition

We begin with a simple example that demonstrates the essential steps of the Par method.

Problem: Given two $n \times n$ matrices a and b, compute their sum:

$$s_{ij} = a_{ij} + b_{ij}, \qquad 1 \le i \le n, \quad 1 \le j \le n$$

3.1.1   The Algorithm

Figure 3.1 contains the obvious algorithm expressed in Par. The first line declares the three matrices. Each is a square matrix of real values. The initialization of a and b has been omitted since it is not of interest here. The concurrent statement closely mirrors the problem specification and is written in a natural parallel fashion.

At this stage many practical considerations are ignored; the goal is to write a clean, understandable program. Hence, the parallelism is expressed in units natural to the algorithm and the three matrices are shared by the parallel chores. However, if each chore in Figure 3.1 were implemented as a separate task (process), the program would be very inefficient on most MIMD computers since the multiprogramming overhead would overwhelm any advantage obtained by concurrent execution. Thus, it is important to combine chores into larger tasks. Moreover, many machines do not have a shared, global memory with uniform access time in which to store the shared objects (the matrices a, b, and s). For NUMA and distributed-memory machines it is thus important to map the data into memory in a way that makes data access local. The remainder of this section shows how these problems can be addressed without sacrificing the simplicity and clarity of the original program.

3.1.2 Adding Scheduling Annotations

Schedulers combine chores into tasks and assign tasks to processors. Combining chores into tasks is essential in this case since the concurrent statement specifies a large number (n^2) of small chores. Since the calculation is entirely predictable, a static scheduler is appropriate.

To minimize the time required to add the two matrices, we want to balance the work among the available processors. This means assigning approximately the same number of chores to each processor. For this problem, any such partition of the chores is equally good. For example, we can divide the array of chores into num_procs bands along the first dimension. Figure 3.2 illustrates the partition of an 8×8 matrix among three processors. The scheduler strip implements this partition.

Using scheduler strip, the concurrent statement of Figure 3.1 is annotated as follows:

```
co i := 1 to n, j := 1 to n {scheduler strip} →
    s[i, j] := a[i, j] + b[i, j]
oc
```

When this annotated concurrent statement is executed, the effect is simultaneously to invoke the scheduler strip once on each processor. It is much as if the following had been written:

```
co processor := low_proc() to high_proc() →
    strip(processor, 1, n, 1, 1, n, 1)
oc
```

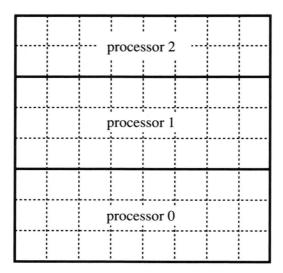

Figure 3.2: An example of the effect of the scheduler strip

(Recall that a scheduler's first argument is the processor number on which it is invoked and that the rest of the arguments are the quantifiers of the concurrent statement.) The instances of strip, collectively, execute **chore** exactly once for each combination of quantifier variables.

Figure 3.3 shows how strip is implemented. Each processor first calculates lower and upper bounds of the rows for which it is responsible, using the standard function **partition**, which partitions an arithmetic progression into pieces. (The function **partition** is given in Appendix A.) Since the bounds are calculated from the number of rows and the number of available processors, the code for the scheduler strip is independent of the number of processors.

To execute one chore of the concurrent statement, the scheduler executes a **chore**

```
scheduler strip(p, l1, u1, s1, l2, u2, s2 : Int)
    my_lb, my_ub : Int :=
                partition(l1, u1, s1, num_procs(), p − min_proc())
    fa  i := my_lb to my_ub by s1, j := l2 to u2 by s2  →
        chore(i, j)
    af
end
```

Figure 3.3: Scheduler Strip.

statement. In the example above, **chore**(i, j) stands for

s[i, j] := a[i, j] + b[i, j]

because this statement forms the body of concurrent statement. In strip, the chores within each task are executed sequentially using a for-all statement.

3.1.3 Adding Mapping Annotations

The next step is to choose mappings for shared objects. The goal is to assign data to processors in such a way that the data resides on the same processor as the task (or tasks) that use it. This is important for efficiency because NUMA computers and multicomputers can access local memory much faster than remote memory.

We think of mappings as preconditions for local access. For each concurrent statement that uses shared data, we add mappings that make the shared objects local to the tasks that use them. In this problem, the best mapping for the shared matrices mirrors the scheduler. The essential point to note is that chore (i, j) accesses element $[i, j]$ of each matrix. Thus, if the matrix elements are partitioned among the processors in exactly the same way as are the chores, all access will be local. To emphasize the close relationship between the mapping and the scheduler, we name the mapping strip also. The concurrent statement is annotated as follows:

```
{map a, b, s : strip}
co i := 1 to n, j := 1 to n {scheduler strip} →
    s[i, j] := a[i, j] + b[i, j]
oc
```

The effect is to specify that each of the matrices is to be mapped using strip. The implementation of the strip mapping is given in Section 3.1.5.

3.1.4 Adding Implementation Annotations

The next step is to annotate declarations of shared abstract data types with concrete resource names. In this case that means picking an implementation for the matrices a, b, and c. For purposes of illustration, we assume that no implementation of Matrix that provides the strip mapping is yet available. In this case StripMatrix seems an appropriate name, so the matrix declaration is annotated as follows:

a, b, s : Matrix⟨Real⟩(1, n, 1, n) {use StripMatrix}

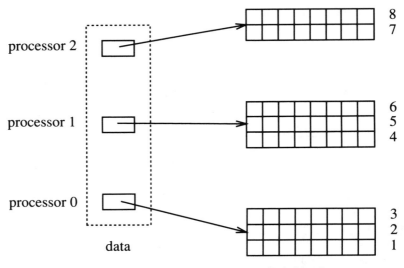

Figure 3.4: Partitioning elements of StripMatrix

The following section describes the implementation of StripMatrix.

In practice, mappings and implementations are not chosen independently; a mapping may be chosen because it is known that an implementation is available. It is possible that the same mapping is provided by several different resources. For example, it is possible that several implementations of Matrix provide the strip mapping, in which case any one of those implementations could be specified.

3.1.5   Implementing StripMatrix

Figure 3.4 illustrates the implementation of StripMatrix in the case of an 8 × 8 matrix and three processors. The original matrix is partitioned into strips along the first dimension. Each processor "owns" a strip of the original matrix, so access to an array element within the local strip is always a local operation.

Figure 3.5 contains an outline of the StripMatrix resource. The specification states that all operations of Matrix are supported, along with the mapping operation strip. The internal representation of a StripMatrix consists of block, which is an instance of IdVector, and several instances of Private. Recall that an instance of IdVector is a vector in which each element resides on a different processor. Each element of block will refer to a block of the partitioned matrix. The objects glb1, etc., are used to store the global bounds of the array; the objects lb1, etc., are used to store the bounds of the block stored by each processor.

Figure 3.6 contains the initial operation. Each processor calculates the size of its

```
resource StripMatrix⟨T⟩
    extends Matrix⟨T⟩
    op strip()
body
    # "block" is a vector of sub-matrices, one per processor.
    # Each sub-matrix represents a strip of the entire matrix
    block : IdVector⟨ref⟨Matrix⟨T⟩⟩⟩
    # Each processor keeps the bounds of the array...
    glb1, gub1, glb2, gub2 : Private⟨Int⟩
    # ...and the bounds of its own block
    lb1, ub1, lb2, ub2 : Private⟨Int⟩
    proc initial... end
    proc assign... end
    proc index... end
    proc strip... end
end StripMatrix
```

Figure 3.5: An outline of StripMatrix

```
proc initial(l1, u1, l2, u2 : Int)
    co p := processors →
        # calculate my lb and ub
        lb1, ub1 := partition(l1, u1, 1, num_procs(), p − low_proc())
        lb2 := l2; ub2 := u2
        # allocate storage for local block
        block ← Matrix⟨T⟩(lb1, ub1, lb2, ub2)
    oc
end
```

Figure 3.6: The initial operation

```
proc index(i, j : Int)
    if  lb1 ≤ i and i ≤ ub1 →
        return block[@][i, j]
    []  else →
        who : Int := owner(glb1, gub1, 1, num_procs(), i)
        return block[who][i, j]
    fi
end
proc assign(i, j : Int, v : T)
    if  lb1 ≤ i and i ≤ ub1 →
        block[@][i, j] := v
    []  else →
        who : Int := owner(glb1, gub1, 1, num_procs(), i)
        block[who][i, j] := v
    fi
end
```

Figure 3.7: The operations index and assign

local block, allocates a matrix of the appropriate size, and initializes the local element of block. The bounds lb1 and lb2 are calculated using the partition function; thus the matrix elements are partitioned in the same way that the scheduler strip partitioned the chores.

Figure 3.7 contains code for the index and assign operations. The operation index(i, j) returns element [i, j], and assign(i, j, value) sets element [i, j] to value. The implementation of the two procedures is similar. Each procedure first checks to see if the indexed element is in the local block. If it is, the operation is performed on the local block (block[@]). If not, the owner of the element is calculated using the owner function (see Appendix A) and the operation is executed on the remote block. In the current example—matrix addition—the remote operations are never used since all access is local. However, other users of StripMatrix might use nonlocal access.

Since StripMatrix supports only one mapping, the data layout is constant and so the operation strip is trivial:

proc strip()**skip end**

When a resource exports more than one mapping the mapping operations are more interesting since they generally involve data movement between processors. In Section 3.4 we expand StripMatrix to support another mapping.

3.1.6 Summary

This section has demonstrated how a clear, machine-independent algorithm can be annotated to yield an efficient program for MIMD computers:

- Section 3.1.1 began with a simple algorithm for matrix addition. The concurrency was expressed in terms of chores: units of parallelism natural to the algorithm. The chores make use of shared objects; no partitioning of the data is specified at this stage.

- In Section 3.1.2 we added scheduling annotations to the concurrent statements. Scheduling annotations combine chores into tasks, which are units of parallelism that can be implemented efficiently on a target computer. Since matrix addition is a regular problem, a static scheduler was used.

- In Section 3.1.3 we added mapping annotations to shared objects to ensure that access to shared objects was local. Locality of access is a prerequisite for efficient implementation on NUMA computers and multicomputers. (If this program were intended only for UMA computers, mapping and implementation annotations could be omitted.)

- In Section 3.1.4 we annotated the declarations of shared objects (in this case matrices) with implementation annotations to specify a concrete implementation, StripMatrix.

- Finally, in Section 3.1.5, we gave an implementation of StripMatrix.

The final program retains the clarity of the original, unannotated version, while also specifying an efficient computation. The architecture-dependent details have been kept separate from the original algorithm; hence they can easily be changed without affecting the correctness of the algorithm. However, the architecture-dependent aspects of the final program are not hidden from the programmer inside a compiler or run-time system, but rather are implemented in Par itself. Hence they can be examined, reused in other programs, or modified if necessary.

3.2 Trapezoidal Integration

This section provides another simple example of the Par method. It also introduces *accumulators,* which provide an efficient parallel implementation of reduction operations (as found in APL [65]) such as summing, or finding the minimum of, a distributed collection of numbers.

```
program trapezoidal
  io : Stdio
  a, b : Real;  n : Int
  io.print("Enter a,b, and n : "); io.read(a, b, n)
  h : (b − a)/(n)
  result : Real(0.0)
  co i := 0 to n →
      if  i = 0 →  result + := f(a)/2.0
      []  i = n →  result + := f(b)/2.0
      []  else →  result + := f(a + i * h)
      fi
  oc
  result * := h
  io.print("the result is ", result)
  # sample function to integrate
   proc f(x : Real) return sin(x) end
end
```

Figure 3.8: Par program for trapezoidal rule.

Problem.   Given a real valued function f of a real parameter, estimate the integral of f over the interval $[a, b]$ by the trapezoidal rule using n sub-intervals:

$$\int_a^b f(x)dx \approx h \left(f(a)/2 + \sum_{i=1}^{n-1} f(a + ih) + f(b)/2 \right)$$

where

$$h = (b − a)/n$$

In this chapter we assume that the time required to evaluate f is constant. If the time required to evaluate f is unpredictable, this algorithm is irregular and requires a dynamic scheduler; this case is discussed in chapter 4.

3.2.1   The Algorithm

Figure 3.8 contains a parallel program for trapezoidal integration. First the constants a, b, n, and h are declared and the real variable result is created with initial value 0.0. Then the sum is calculated. Since the elements of the sum are independent of one another, they are calculated in parallel. Finally, the result is printed.

```
scheduler block(p, l1, u1, s1 : Int)
    my_lb, my_ub : Int :=
            partition(l1, u1, s1, num_procs(), p − min_proc())
    fa i := my_lb to my_ub by s1 →
        chore(i)
    af
end
```

Figure 3.9: Scheduler Block.

3.2.2 Adding Scheduling Annotations

Since the time required to evaluate f is assumed to be constant, load balancing can be achieved by partitioning the chores into equal-sized tasks and assigning one task to each processor. This could be done in many ways. We choose to reuse the scheduler block, which was introduced in Chapter 1 (page 6). This provides an opportunity to show the implementation of block and also illustrates the fact that Zschedulers are amenable to reuse.

The implementation of the scheduler block is shown in Figure 3.9. Each processor calculates the bounds on the block of chores for which it is responsible and then it iterates through that block, executing each chore in turn.

3.2.3 Adding Implementation Annotations

In this program the shared objects are the numbers a, b, n, h, and result. The first four are calculated once and never modified thereafter; hence they will be replicated on all processors. (See section 5.1.2 for how this is accomplished.) However, the real number result presents a problem. If it were implemented as a single memory cell, it would have to reside in a single memory module. On NUMA computers and multicomputers, access to result would be remote from all processors except one. Moreover, since only one task at a time could access the cell, a bottleneck would result. (This kind of memory bottleneck on UMA and NUMA computers is often called a *hot spot*.) Clearly this situation is not acceptable.

However, a distributed implementation is suggested by the rather specialized way in which result is used. First result is initialized to 0.0, the identity element of the sum operation. Thereafter, the only operation applied to result is sum_assign (+:=). Objects that are used in this way are termed accumulators. What is needed is a resource that provides a parallel implementation of a real-valued accumulator. We call this resource AccRealSum and annotate the declaration of result as follows:

result : Real(0.0) {use AccRealSum}

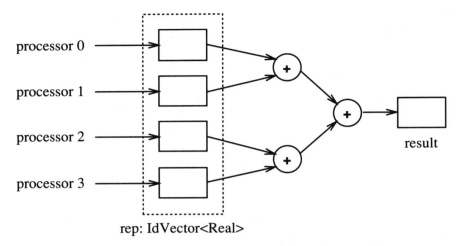

rep: IdVector<Real>

Figure 3.10: Implementation of the accumulator AccRealSum

The implementation of AccRealSum, and accumulators in general, is discussed in the following section.

3.2.4   Implementing Accumulators

A common programming task is to accumulate a number of values by a commutative, associative operation. In the current example, the operation is sum. Other operations that are commonly used this way include **and, or**, product, min, and max. For example, the code fragment

```
bres : Bool(false)
co i := 1 to n →  bres or := v[i] oc
```

accumulates the conjunction of the elements of the boolean vector v into bres. The boolean variable bres is initialized to false—the identity element of the **or** operation—and the only operation applied to it is or_assign, which is commutative and associative.

Accumulators have an efficient parallel implementation because commutativity and associativity of the operator allow the elements to be combined in any order. Thus we can take advantage of locality of reference to minimize the number of remote operations. Figure 3.10 illustrates the idea. The actual value of the variable is not "known" by any one processor; instead it is distributed across the processors. The sum_assign operation accumulates the values into the local element of piece. When the final result is needed, the rep operation combines the partial results and reports the answer.

```
resource AccRealSum
    extends Real
body
    piece : IdVector⟨Real⟩
    proc Real
        abort("Operation not supported on accumulator")
    end
    proc initial(r : Real)
        co p := processors →
            piece[p] := r
        oc
    end
    proc sum_assign(r : Real)
        piece[@] + := r
    end
    proc rep()
        result : Real
        co p := processors →
            result + := piece[p]
        oc
        return result.rep()
    end
end AccRealSum
```

Figure 3.11: An accumulator for real sums.

The implementation of AccRealSum is shown in Figure 3.11. In the initial operation, all the processors set their element of piece to the initial value. The sum_assign operation adds its parameter to the current processor's element of piece. This operation is local. The rep operation accumulates the results from all the processors into an ordinary real number and returns the representation of that real number. (For simplicity, this version does not implement the "tree of sums" strategy shown in Figure 3.10; instead it simply adds all the partial results to result.) Finally, procedure Real implements the remaining operations of Real by issuing an error message and aborting the computation. The same technique can be used to program accumulators for other commutative, associative operations.

```
a, b, c : Matrix⟨Real⟩(1, n, 1, n)
# initialize "a" and "b"
co i := 1 to n, j := 1 to n →
    c[i, j] := 0.0
    co k := 1 to n →
        c[i, j] + := a[i, k] * b[k, j]
    oc
oc
```

Figure 3.12: Matrix Multiplication

3.3   Matrix Multiplication

This example illustrates the use of data replication to decrease access time. It also introduces the use of *virtual architectures,* which are used to isolate architecture-dependent details from the main program.

Problem: Given two $n \times n$ matrices a and b, find their matrix product c:

$$c_{ij} = \sum_{k=1}^{n} a_{ik} b_{kj}, \qquad 1 \le i \le n, \quad 1 \le j \le n$$

Figure 3.12 shows the basic algorithm for matrix multiplication in its most obvious form. The program closely follows the problem statement. Each element of the result is the dot product of two vectors—one a row of a, the other a column of b. The dot products are independent and can be computed in parallel. There is also potential for parallelism within the calculation of each dot product. The goal at this stage is to express the maximum amount of parallelism; it can always be removed later by adding schedulers.

3.3.1   Virtual Architectures

In the following sections we will find it convenient to think of the processors on a parallel computer as arranged in a rectangular grid. For example, Figure 3.13 shows one way a sixteen-processor multicomputer could be arranged as a 4×4 grid. The natural way to name processors in a grid is by grid coordinates rather than processor number. For example, grid(2, 3) is the natural way to name processor 14 in Figure 3.13. Thus it is useful to be able to translate back and forth between processor numbers and grid coordinates.

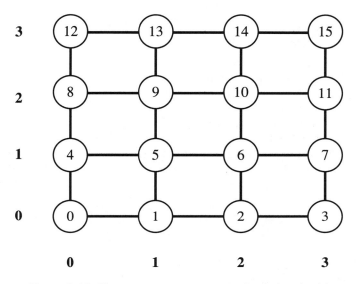

Figure 3.13: Sixteen processors arranged as a 4×4 grid

A *virtual architecture* is a resource that encapsulates the translation between a virtual arrangement of processors—such as the grid above—and the physical processor numbers. Figure 3.14 contains an implementation of the virtual architecture Grid for a sixteen-processor parallel computer. It provides the operations width and height, which return the width and height of the grid; the operation grid, which translates from processor number to grid coordinates; and processor, which translates from grid coordinates to processor numbers.

Note that the implementation of Grid is not portable; indeed, it is highly dependent on details of the computer architecture. However, using virtual architectures increases the portability of programs since all the details that depend on the architecture are confined to the implementation of the virtual architecture. Programs that use a virtual architecture can be ported to new computers by merely reimplementing the virtual architecture; there is no need to change the program itself.

To use a virtual architecture, a program creates an instance of it and uses the exported operations. In this example, the declaration

{g : Grid}

is added to the beginning of the program in Figure 3.12. The declaration of g is enclosed in braces because the use of g is confined to other annotations.

```
resource Grid
    op width() returns Int;
    op height() return Int;
    op grid(Int) returns Int, Int
    op processor(Int, Int) returns Int
body
    proc width() return 4 end
    proc height() return 4 end
    proc grid(p : Int) return(p mod 4, p div 4)
    proc processor(i, j) return i + 4 * j
end
```

Figure 3.14: The virtual architecture Grid

```
scheduler block(p, l1, u1, s1, l2, u2, s2 : Int)
    # calculate my block boundaries
    x, y : Int := g.grid(p)
    my_xmin, my_xmax : Int := partition(l1, u1, s1, g.width(), x)
    my_ymin, my_ymax : Int := partition(l2, u2, s2, g.height(), y)
    # iterate over chores in my block
    fa  i := my_xmin to my_xmax, j := my_ymin to my_xmax →
        chore(i, j)
    af
end
```

Figure 3.15: The scheduler block.

3.3.2   Adding Scheduling Annotations

The concurrent statement in Figure 3.12 represents an $n \times n$ matrix of chores. One simple way to assign chores to processes is to partition the matrix of chores into blocks and assign each block to a processor.

Figure 3.15 contains an implementation of the scheduler block . Each processor calculates its block boundaries and executes the chores in its block sequentially. The block boundaries are calculated using the virtual architecture and the partition function.[1] The outer concurrent statement provides a high degree of parallelism. Furthermore, the chores of the inner concurrent statement are very small. Thus we anno-

---

[1]Recall that we used the name "block" to refer to a different scheduler in Chapter 1. The two uses of the name do not conflict, however, because the two schedulers are parameterized differently.

tate the inner concurrent statement to combine all the chores into one task using the built-in scheduler forall:

```
co k := 1 to n    {scheduler forall} →
   c[i, j] + := a[i, k] * b[k, j]
oc
```

As described in Section 2.10.2, the scheduler forall has the effect of implementing the concurrent statement as a for-all statement. Thus the dot product is implemented as if it had been written as follows:

```
fa k := 1 to n →
   c[i, j] + := a[i, k] * b[k, j]
af
```

Although the decision made here—to combine all the chores of the inner concurrent statement into one task—is a reasonable one, it is not the only possibility. For example, on computers that can execute fine-grained computations efficiently, a different scheduler could be used.

3.3.3 Adding Mapping and Implementation Annotations

With the scheduling strategy shown above, each processor is responsible for a block of chores and thus for a block of elements of the result matrix. Also, neither a nor b is modified during the calculation. In general, mapping read-only objects is easy because pieces can be duplicated.

These considerations lead naturally to mappings for c, a and b. The matrix c is partitioned into blocks in the same way that the chores are. Since chore (i, j) modifies only c[i, j], access to c will be local. Each block of the result matrix depends on a horizontal strip of a and a vertical strip of b. Thus elements in a horizontal strip of a and a vertical strip of b are replicated on each processor that requires them. The mapping for matrix a is called row_dup and the mapping for matrix b is called col_dup.

Figure 3.16 contains the fully-annotated version of the matrix multiplication algorithm. We have chosen to call the concrete resource BlockMatrix. The implementation of BlockMatrix is described in the following section.

```
{g : Grid}
c, a, b : Matrix⟨Real⟩ {use BlockMatrix}
{map a : row_dup, b : col_dup, c : block}
co i := 1 to n, j := 1 to n {scheduler block} →
    c[i, j] := 0.0
    co k := 1 to n {scheduler forall} →
        c[i, j] + := a[i, k] * b[k, j]
    oc
oc
```

Figure 3.16: Fully annotated code for matrix multiplication

```
resource BlockMatrix⟨T⟩
    extends Matrix⟨T⟩
    op block()
    op row_dup()
    op col_dup()
body
    # current mapping
    enum(block_map, row_map, col_map)
    mapping : Private⟨Int⟩
    # global matrix bounds
    glb1, gub1, glb2, gub3 : Private⟨Int⟩
    # storage and bounds for the local block
    bl : IdVector⟨ref⟨Matrix⟨T⟩⟩⟩
    lb1, lb2, ub1, ub2 : Private⟨Int⟩
    # storage for replicated rows and columns
    row, col : IdVector⟨ref⟨Matrix⟨T⟩⟩⟩
    # Matrix operations
    proc initial.. end
    proc index... end
    proc assign.. end
    # mapping operations
    proc block...en
    proc row_dup... end
    proc col_dup...en
end BlockMatrix
```

Figure 3.17: Resource BlockMatrix

```
proc initial(l1, u1, l2, u2 : Int)
    co p := processors →
        glb1 := l1; gub1 := u1; glb2 := l2; gub2 := u2
        x, y : Int := g.grid(p)
        lb1, ub1 := partition(l1, u1, 1, g.width(), x)
        lb2, ub2 := partition(l2, u2, 1, g.height(), y)
        bl ← Vector⟨T⟩(lb1, ub1, lb2, ub2)
    oc
end
```

Figure 3.18: The initial operation

3.3.4 Implementing Concrete Resources

The resource BlockMatrix extends Matrix with the three mapping operations block, row_dup, and col_dup. Figure 3.17 contains an outline of the implementation of BlockMatrix. The internal representation is an IdVector of matrix blocks, two instances of IdVector to store the replicated rows and columns, and some private variables to store block bounds.

Figure 3.18 contains the initial operation. Each processor first saves the global bounds of the matrix, then calculates the bounds on its local block and allocates that block. The bounds are calculated in terms of the virtual architecture. As explained below, memory for replicated rows and columns is allocated in the appropriate mapping operations when it is needed.

Figure 3.19 contains the assign and index operations. The assign operation modifies the appropriate element in the local block. If the index is nonlocal, or if the mapping is not block, the computation is aborted. The index operation retrieves a value from the appropriate place, depending on which mapping is in effect.

Our algorithm never modifies an element of a matrix that is in the row_dup or col_dup mappings, and it never attempts to access nonlocal matrix elements. Thus we have chosen to implement assign and index so that they simply abort with a warning message if nonlocal access is attempted. Nonlocal access could be implemented, but it would add considerably to the complexity of these two procedures. In general, it is permissible for a concrete resource to restrict the semantics of the abstract data type it implements. This may be desirable either for simplicity or efficiency. However, a concrete resource should never produce an erroneous result; it should either faithfully implement the semantics of the abstract data type or else issue an error message.

Figure 3.20 contains the mappings block and row_dup. The mapping block merely records the fact that the current mapping is block. The mapping row_dup first allocates space for replicated rows if this has not already been done. Then a barrier is executed

```
proc assign(i, j : Int, value : T)
    if   mapping = block_map →
         bl[i, j] := value
    []   else →
         abort("assignment in shared mapping")
    fi
end
proc index(i, j : Int)
    if   mapping = block_map  →  return bl[i, j]
    []   mapping = row_map    →  return row[i, j]
    []   mapping = col_map    →  return col[i, j]
    fi
end
```

Figure 3.19: The assign and index operations

```
proc block()
    co p := processors →
       mapping := block_map
    oc
end
proc row_dup()
    co p := processors →
       # if rows have not yet been allocated, allocate them
       if   null(row) →
            row ← Matrix⟨T⟩(glb1, gub1, lb2, ub2)
       fi
       barrier
       # copy my block to all processors in my row ("x")
       x, y : Int := g.grid(p)
       fa i := 0 to g.width() − 1 →
          who : Int := g.processor(x, i)
          row[who][lb1 : ub1, lb2 : ub2] := bl
       af
    oc
end
```

Figure 3.20: The mapping operations

to ensure that all the processors have allocated memory for replicated rows before the assignments take place. Finally, each processor copies its local block to each of the processors in its row of the virtual grid. (Chapter 5 describes how remote assignment can be implemented on various kinds of MIMD computers.) The mapping col_dup is entirely analogous to row_dup; for the sake of brevity it has been omitted.

3.4 Region Labeling

The example of this section combines several features from earlier examples and also illustrates the use of remapping.

Problem: We are given an $n \times n$ array of pixels. Each pixel has a color, represented by an integer. The *neighbors* of a pixel are the eight pixels that surround it. (Pixels on the edge of the image have fewer than eight neighbors, of course.) A set of pixels is connected if, for any two pixels p and q in the set, a chain of pixels $(p = p_0, p_1, \ldots p_k = q)$ exists such that the entire chain lies in the set, and such that p_i and p_{i+1} are neighbors for $0 \leq i < k$. A maximal connected set of identically colored pixels is called a *region*. The problem is to read an image, assign a different integer label to each region, and write the label that corresponds to each pixel.

3.4.1 The Algorithm

One natural algorithm to solve this problem is iterative. The pixels are initially given unique labels, e.g., pixel (i, j) is labeled $n \times i + j$. During each iteration the labels are propagated to neighboring pixels that have the same color but smaller labels. In each iteration, the new labels for all the pixels can be calculated simultaneously. The algorithm terminates when the labels stop changing, so each pixel is ultimately labeled with the largest label in its region.

Figure 3.21 contains the main program for region labeling. First the image size is read and three arrays are declared. (To simplify the program, the arrays are surrounded by a border one pixel wide.) The label array is initialized. Then the main algorithm is executed, as described above. It follows a common model: calculate, check for termination, and prepare for the next iteration. Finally, the values of the labels are printed.

Figure 3.22 contains the procedures initialize_labels, calculate, different, and copy, each implemented in a natural parallel style. The procedure initialize_labels assigns unique labels to all pixels. Since these are independent calculations, they are specified as concurrent chores. Procedure calculate computes, for each pixel, a new label based on the current label and the labels of surrounding pixels with the same value. Again, the pixel labels can be updated in parallel so a concurrent statement

```
program label_regions
   n : int; prompt("size? "); read(n)
   image, label, new_label : Matrix⟨Int⟩(0, n + 1, 0, n + 1)
   read_image(image)
   # assign unique labels to label.
   initialize_labels()
   # main algorithm: iterate until labels don't change
   changed : Bool(true)
   do changed →
      calculate()
      changed := different()
      if  changed  →  copy() fi
   od
   # print results
   write_labels(label)
end
```

Figure 3.21: The main program for region labeling

is used. In similar parallel fashion, different compares the new and old labels of all pixels and copy prepares for the next iteration by copying new_label to label.

3.4.2   Adding Scheduler Annotations

For each procedure in Figure 3.22, a natural way to partition the chores is into contiguous blocks or strips. Since a scheduler strip has already been implemented (Section 3.1.2) we will reuse it here. Figure 3.23 shows how initialize_labels can be annotated; the other procedures are annotated similarly and are omitted for the sake of brevity.

3.4.3   Adding Mapping Annotations

The next step is to choose mappings for the shared data objects. Each procedure is considered separately.

The procedures initialize_labels and copy are trivial. The only shared objects are the arrays label and new_label. Furthermore, chore (i, j) accesses only element $[i, j]$ of these matrices. Thus element $[i, j]$ of each array is mapped to the processor that executes the chore $[i, j]$. This is accomplished by the mapping strip introduced in Section 3.1.3. Figure 3.24 shows these two procedures with mapping annotations.

```
# assign distinct labels to pixels; set border to zero
proc initialize_labels()
    co i := 0 to n + 1, j := 0 to n + 1 →
        if  i = 0 or j = 0 →  label[i, j] = 0
        []  i = n + 1 or j = n + 1 →  label[i, j] = 0
        []  else →  label[i, j] := i * n + j
        fi
    oc
end
# calculate new value for each pixel
proc calculate()
    co i := 1 to n, j := 1 to n →
        new_label[i, j] := label[i, j]
        fa  x := i − 1 to i + 1, y := j − 1 to j + 1 →
            if  image[i, j] = image[x, y] →
                new_label[i, j] := max(label[i, j], label[x, y])
            fi
        af
    oc
end
# return true iff " label" and " new_label" differ
proc different()
    result : Bool(false)
    co i := 1 to n, j := 1 to n →
        result or := label[i, j] ≠ new_label[i, j]
    oc
    return result
end
# copy " new_label" into " label"
proc copy()
    co i := 1 to n, j := 1 to n →
        label[i, j] := new_label[i, j]
    oc
end
```

Figure 3.22: Parallel implementation of labeling procedures.

```
# assign distinct labels to pixels; set border to zero
proc initialize_labels()
    co i := 0 to n + 1, j := 0 to n + 1 {scheduler strip} →
        if  i mod n + 1 = 0 or j mod n + 1 = 0 →  label[i, j] = 0
        []   else →  label[i, j] := i * n + j
        fi
    oc
end
```

Figure 3.23: Adding a scheduling annotation to initialize_labels.

```
proc initialize_labels()
    {map label.strip}
    co i := 0 to n + 1, j := 0 to n + 1 {scheduler strip} →
        if  i mod n = 0 or j mod n = 0 →  label[i, j] := 0
        []   else →  label[i, j] := i * n + j
        fi
    oc
end
proc copy()
    {map label.strip, new_label.strip}
    co i := 1 to n, j := 1 to n {scheduler strip} →
        label[i, j] := new_label[i, j]
    oc
end
```

Figure 3.24: The two easy mappings.

```
# calculate new value for each pixel based on surrounding pixels
proc calculate()
    {map image.shared_edges, label.shared_edges, new_label.strip}
    co i := 1 to n, j := 1 to n {scheduler strip} →
        new_label[i, j] := label[i, j]
        fa x := i − 1 to i + 1, y := j − 1 to j + 1 →
            if image[i, j] = image[x, y] →
                new_label[i, j] := max(label[i, j], label[x, y])
            fi
        af
    oc
end
```

Figure 3.25: Annotated version of calculate.

The procedure calculate is somewhat more complicated because the array cannot be partitioned in such a way that all tasks are completely local. This is because the label of each pixel depends on the eight pixels that surround it; no matter how the pixels are partitioned, the labels of pixels on the partition boundaries will depend on pixels in a different partition (and thus on another processor). If the mapping strip is used the program will perform poorly on computers that have a high remote-access time. This problem can be resolved quite simply because the shared items (the array cells that lie on the boundary of a strip) are not modified in calculate. Thus a mapping shared_edges is introduced in which the cells on the edge of the strips are replicated on both the processors that access them.

While the mapping of a matrix is shared_edges, reading cells on the shared border is a local operation—the local value is used. However, modifying such cells is nonlocal because both cells must be changed atomically to maintain the commonly-understood semantics of a matrix. (A possible protocol is to lock both cells, modify them, and then unlock them. This requires that several messages pass between the two processors.)

It is important to note, however, that in this algorithm elements of a matrix are only read while the mapping of the matrix is shared_edges and only written while the mapping is strip. Indeed, this is the point of a mapping annotation—to modify the representation of a data structure so that certain operations are less expensive.

Figure 3.25 shows procedure calculate annotated with the shared_edges mapping. In Section 3.4.5 we expand the implementation of StripMatrix to provide both strip and shared_edges.

Finally, consider the procedure different. The matrices label and new_label are mapped using strip since cross-partition access is not needed. The boolean variable result is used as a boolean accumulator; this is discussed further in the next two sections.

3.4.4 Annotating Declarations of Shared Objects

Again, we need to annotate declarations of shared abstract data types with concrete resource names. In this case that means picking an implementation for the matrices and the boolean variable result in the procedure different. For purposes of illustration, we will assume that no implementation of Matrix that provides both strip and shared_edges is available in a library. Thus we will rewrite the resource StripMatrix to implement both mappings. The matrix declaration is annotated as follows:

$$\text{image, label, new\_label} : \text{Matrix}\langle\text{Int}\rangle(0, n + 1, 0, n + 1)$$
$$\{\text{use StripMatrix}\}$$

We further assume that no parallel implementation of a boolean accumulator is yet available; this concrete resource will be called AccOr and the declaration of result is annotated as follows:

$$\text{result} : \text{Bool}(\text{false}) \ \{\text{use AccOr}\}$$

3.4.5 Implementing Concrete Resources

This section discusses the implementation of StripMatrix. The resource AccOr is almost identical to AccRealSum, which was explained in Section 3.2.4.

Figure 3.26 illustrates the implementation of StripMatrix in the case of an 8×8 matrix and three processors. The original matrix is partitioned into strips along the first dimension. Each processor "owns" a strip of the original matrix, so access to an array element within the local strip is always a local operation.

Each processor keeps extra rows to store the bordering edges of the strips above and below, and also keeps track of whether its extra rows currently contain valid information. For example, processor 1 owns rows 4–6, but also allocates space for the top and bottom border rows 7 and 3. When shared is true, the extra rows are considered valid, and access to the corresponding indices is a local operation; when shared is false, the extra rows are ignored and access to indices corresponding to the extra rows is done remotely. (In the region labeling algorithm, remote access will never occur since all the interprocessor communication is accomplished by the mapping shared_edges.) Figure 3.27 contains an outline of the resource StripMatrix.

In the initial operation, shown in Figure 3.28, each processor calculates the size of its local array, including the two extra rows described above, and initializes the local

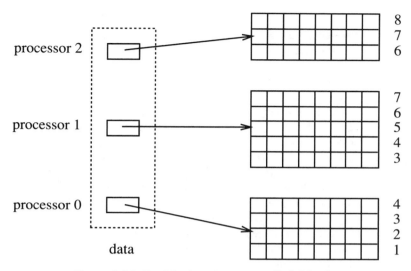

Figure 3.26: Partitioning elements of StripMatrix

element of block. At the end of initial each processor sets its **shared** flag to false to indicate that the extra rows do not contain valid information since the initial mapping is strip.

Figure 3.29 contains the procedures assign and index. Our algorithm never modifies an element of a matrix that is in the shared_edges mapping, and it never attempts to access nonlocal matrix elements. Thus we have chosen to implement assign and index so that they simply abort with a warning message if either is attempted.

Figure 3.30 contains the mapping procedures. The implementation of strip is trivial: each processor sets **shared** to false so that the extra rows are ignored. The procedure shared_edges is implemented by exchanging edges between neighbors and then setting **shared** to true. This procedure is the only place in which the border rows are modified. The exchange of edges is accomplished by remote assignment. (This will be implemented by a block move on a computer with shared memory or by message passing on a multicomputer; see Chapter 5.)

3.5 Gaussian Elimination

This section illustrates the use of more interesting schedulers and mappings to achieve load balancing.

```
resource StripMatrix⟨T⟩
    extends Matrix⟨T⟩
    op strip()
    op shared_edges()
body
    # "block" is a vector of sub-matrices, one per processor.
    # Each sub-matrix represents a strip of the entire matrix
    block : Private⟨Matrix⟨T⟩⟩
    # Each processor keeps the bounds of its own block
    lb1, ub2, lb2, ub2 : Private⟨Int⟩
    # When "shared" is true, the edges have been exchanged
    # and cross-border references are local. When "shared"
    # is false, the current edges have not been exchanged;
    # cross-border references must be done remotely.
    shared : Private⟨Bool⟩
    proc initial... end
    proc assign... end
    proc index... end
    proc strip... end
    proc shared_edges... end
end StripMatrix
```

Figure 3.27: The internal representation of StripMatrix

```
proc initial(l1, u1, l2, u2 : Int)
    co p := processors →
        # calculate my lb and ub
        lb1, ub1 := partition(l1, u1, 1, num_procs(), p − low_proc())
        lb2 := l2
        ub2 := u2
        # allocate storage for local matrix, including borders
        block ← Matrix⟨T⟩(lb1 − 1, ub1 + 1, lb2, ub2)
        # the initial mapping is "strip"
        shared := false
    oc
end
```

Figure 3.28: The initial operation

```
proc assign(i, j : Int, value : T)
    if  not shared and lb1 ≤ i and i ≤ ub1 →
        block[i, j] := value
    []  else →
        abort("assignment in shared mapping")
    fi
end
proc index(i, j : Int)
    if  lb1 ≤ i and i ≤ ub1 →  return block[i, j]
    []  shared and (i = lb1 − 1 or i = ub1 + 1) →  return block[i, j]
    []  else →
        abort("nonlocal access")
    fi
end
```

Figure 3.29: The procedures assign and index

```
proc strip()
    co p := processors →
        shared := false
    oc
end
proc shared_edges()
    co p := processors →
        if  not shared →
            block[p − 1][lb, lb2 : ub2] := block[p][lb, lb2 : ub2]
            block[p + 1][ub, lb2 : ub2] := block[p][ub, lb2 : ub2]
            shared := true
        fi
    oc
end
```

Figure 3.30: The procedures strip and shared_edges

Problem: Given a, an $n \times n$ matrix of real numbers, reduce it to upper-triangular form by Gaussian elimination using partial pivoting.

3.5.1 The Algorithm

We first describe the standard sequential algorithm for Gaussian elimination with partial pivoting. Briefly, the algorithm iterates down the main diagonal of the matrix a. For each diagonal element a_{dd} it zeros the elements in the column below the diagonal element. This is done in three steps:

1. A pivot row is found. For a diagonal element a_{dd}, the pivot is the element of the set $\{a_{dd}, a_{d+1,d}, \ldots, a_{nd}\}$ with the maximum absolute value. For example, consider the matrix

$$\begin{bmatrix} 2.3 & 3.5 & 9.8 & -3.4 \\ -3.4 & 5.6 & -3.0 & 6.7 \\ 7.0 & 1.2 & -2.0 & -1.3 \\ 2.4 & -5.6 & -10.0 & 1.3 \end{bmatrix}$$

   The pivot element corresponding to a_{11} is 7.0. The pivot row is the row that contains the pivot element; in this case the pivot row is 3.

2. The pivot row and the diagonal row are exchanged. In the example, a is transformed to

$$\begin{bmatrix} 7.0 & 1.2 & -2.0 & -1.3 \\ -3.4 & 5.6 & -3.0 & 6.7 \\ 2.3 & 3.5 & 9.8 & -3.4 \\ 2.4 & -5.6 & -10.0 & 1.3 \end{bmatrix}$$

3. Each row r_i, $d < i \leq n$, is replaced by $r_i - f \cdot r_d$, where $f = a_{id}/a_{dd}$. This has the effect of making the elements $a_{d+1,d}, \ldots, a_{nd}$ zero. In the example, r_2 is replaced by $r_2 - (-3.4/7.0)r_1$. This yields the matrix

$$\begin{bmatrix} 7.0 & 1.2 & -2.0 & -1.3 \\ 0.0 & 6.18 & -3.97 & 6.07 \\ 2.3 & 3.5 & 9.8 & -3.4 \\ 2.4 & -5.6 & -10.0 & 1.3 \end{bmatrix}$$

Similarly, row 3 is replaced by $r_3 - (2.3/7.0)r_1$ and row 4 is replaced by $r_4 - (2.4/7.0)r_1$:

$$\begin{bmatrix} 7.0 & 1.2 & -2.0 & -1.3 \\ 0.0 & 6.18 & -3.97 & 6.07 \\ 0.0 & 3.10 & 10.46 & -2.97 \\ 0.0 & -6.01 & -9.31 & 1.75 \end{bmatrix}$$

This completes the first iteration of the main loop. The second iteration repeats the same three steps with $d = 2$. The pivot row is 2, so the exchange has no effect. Rows 3 and 4 are replaced by $r_3 - (3.10/6.18)r_2$ and $r_4 - (-6.01/6.18)r_2$, respectively, yielding

$$\begin{bmatrix} 7.0 & 1.2 & -2.0 & -1.3 \\ 0.0 & 6.18 & -3.97 & 6.07 \\ 0.0 & 0.0 & 12.45 & -6.02 \\ 0.0 & 0.0 & -13.18 & 7.65 \end{bmatrix}$$

This completes the second iteration.

In the final iteration, the three steps are repeated with $d = 3$. The pivot row is 4. Thus rows 3 and 4 are exchanged, yielding

$$\begin{bmatrix} 7.0 & 1.2 & -2.0 & -1.3 \\ 0.0 & 6.18 & -3.97 & 6.07 \\ 0.0 & 0.0 & -13.18 & 7.65 \\ 0.0 & 0.0 & 12.45 & -6.02 \end{bmatrix}$$

Then row 4 is replaced by $r_4 - (12.45/-13.18)r_3$, yielding the final result:

$$\begin{bmatrix} 7.0 & 1.2 & -2.0 & -1.3 \\ 0.0 & 6.18 & -3.97 & 6.07 \\ 0.0 & 0.0 & -13.18 & 7.65 \\ 0.0 & 0.0 & 0.0 & 1.20 \end{bmatrix}$$

A more detailed explanation of the sequential algorithm for Gaussian elimination (including some bookkeeping that is ignored here but is usually necessary in real applications) can be found in most numerical analysis books. An important point to note is that in each iteration of the main loop one column is completed and thus becomes dormant for the rest of the computation.

Figure 3.31 contains a parallel algorithm for Gaussian elimination. It closely follows the sequential algorithm. The outer loop is sequential. However, in steps two and three of the sequential algorithm, independent calculations are done; these are expressed as concurrent statements.

3.5.2 Adding Mapping Annotations

The elimination step, where row r of the matrix is modified according to the formula

$$a[r, 1 : n] := a[r, 1 : n] - factor * a[d, 1 : n]$$

is the part of this program where the most parallelism is potentially available. This chore uses only two rows plus the real number *factor*. To achieve a high degree of

```
program gauss
    io : Stdio
    n : Int; io.read(n)
    a : Matrix⟨Real⟩(1, n, 1, n)
    # read "a"
    ...
    fa d := 1 to n →
        # select pivot
        pivot : Int := a[d, d]
        pivot_row : Int := d
        fa row := d to n →
            if  a[row, d] > pivot →
                pivot := a[row, d]
                pivot_row := row
            fi
        af
        if  pivot = 0.0 →  abort("Matrix is singular") fi
        # swap rows
        co col := d to n →
            temp : Real := a[pivot_row, col]
            a[pivot_row, col] := a[d, col]
            a[d, col] := temp
        oc
        # calculate "factor" and do elimination
        co row := d + 1 to n →
            factor : Real := a[row, d]/pivot
            # elimination
            co col := d + 1 to n →
                a[row, col]− := factor * a[row, d]
            oc
        oc
    af
end
```

Figure 3.31: Gaussian elimination with partial pivoting

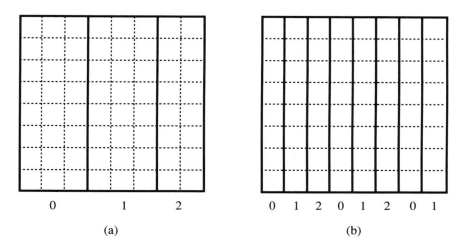

Figure 3.32: Two ways to assign matrix columns to processors

parallelism, these rows must be distributed across all the processors. Thus the obvious way to map the matrix a is to partition it by columns.

Figure 3.32(a) shows one way to assign columns of a matrix to processors, illustrated with an 8×8 matrix and 3 processors. However, this mapping is not quite what is needed, since the active part of the matrix shrinks as the computation proceeds. In the first iteration of the outer loop all columns are active; in the last iteration only the last column is active. If the matrix were partitioned as in Figure 3.32(a), the processors assigned to the left-hand columns would become idle soon after the calculation started. A better way to map the matrix is termed *scattered decomposition* [88] and is illustrated in Figure 3.32(b). Here the columns are mapped to processors in cyclic fashion so each processor owns columns all across the matrix. This allows the work load to remain balanced among the processors; all the processors continue to participate in the calculation until the final few iterations of the outer loop.

The resource ScatteredColMatrix provides this mapping; the implementation will be given in Section 3.5.4.

3.5.3   Adding Scheduling Annotations

Figure 3.31 contains three concurrent statements to be scheduled. Consider first the statement that swaps rows:

```
scheduler col_sched(p, l, u, s : Int)
    fa  c := l to u by s →
        if  (c − lb1) mod num_procs() = p →
            chore(c)
        fi
    af
end
```

Figure 3.33: The schedulers col_sched

```
co i := d to n →
    temp : Real := a[d, i]
    a[d, i] := a[pivot_row, i]
    a[pivot_row, i] := temp
oc
```

The chores can be made local to the data they use by scheduling chore i on the processor that owns column i. This scheduler is called col_sched, since it is used to iterate across columns. Figure 3.33 contains an implementation of col_sched. Each processor iterates through the quantifier range and executes those chores that are local.

Next consider the nested concurrent statments:

```
co row := d + 1 to n →
    factor : Real := a[row, d]/pivot
    # elimination
    co col := d + 1 to n →
        a[row, col]− := factor ∗ a[row, d]
    oc
oc
```

The outer concurrent statement contains one chore for each row d+1..n, while the inner concurrent statement contains one chore for each column d + 1..n. The inner concurrent statement can conveniently be scheduled using col_sched, saving the trouble of writing another scheduler. If n is large compared to the number of processors, the inner concurrent statement will exhibit enough parallelism for most parallel computers. Thus the outer concurrent statement is annotated with the scheduler forall, which has the effect of implementing it as a for-all statement.

It may seem counterintuitive that the outer concurrent statement is executed sequentially while the inner one is executed in parallel. The advantage to scheduling the inner statement in parallel is that its chores access matrix elements that are conveniently distributed across the processors so that col_sched makes all the chores local.

3.5.4 Implementing Concrete Resources

An implementation of ScatteredColMatrix is shown in Figure 3.34. The implementation is similar to previous examples. In the initial operation, each processor stores the array bounds and allocates a sub-matrix to store its columns. The index procedure first checks to see if the requested element is local. If so, it returns a local element; if not, it computes the owner and returns a remote element. The assign operation is similar.

3.6 Sorting

Problem: Given a vector of integers, permute them so they appear in non-decreasing order.

3.6.1 The Algorithm

There are many parallel algorithms for sorting; in this section we consider a class of algorithms based on compare-exchange sorting. Compare-exchange algorithms sort by engaging in a series of compare-exchange steps, each of which compares two element and perhaps exchanges them based on the comparison. Shellsort, merge-exchange sort, and bitonic sort are examples of compare-exchange sorts. None of these algorithms makes a good MIMD sorting algorithm because none exhibits good locality of reference. As a consequence, it impossible to take advantage of the fact that MIMD computers can sort local elements very efficiently using standard sequential algorithms.

However any compare-exchange sorting algorithm can be adapted to provide more locality of reference by the following trick [48]. The array to be sorted is divided into blocks. Each block is sorted using any sequential algorithm. Then the compare-exchange algorithm is executed, but the units of sorting are array blocks instead of individual array elements. Also, instead of comparing and exchanging the two blocks, the elements of the two blocks are merged and then split; the higher elements going to one block, the lower to the other.

To clarify this algorithm transformation, consider the odd-even transposition sort. This algorithm performs compare-exchange steps only on adjacent elements; in odd-numbered steps element 1 is compared and perhaps exchanged with element 2, element 3 with 4, etc. In even numbered steps elements 2 and 3, 4 and 5, etc. are compared and perhaps exchanged. This algorithm is guaranteed to sort n elements in n steps. For example, consider the vector

$$\begin{bmatrix} 4 & 2 & 3 & 1 \end{bmatrix}$$

```
resource ScatteredColMatrix⟨T⟩
    extends Matrix⟨T⟩
body
    piece : IdVector⟨ref⟨Matrix⟨T⟩⟩⟩
    lb1, ub1, lb2, ub2 : Private⟨Int⟩
    proc initial(l1, u1, l2, u2 : Int)
        co p := processors →
            # save matrix bounds
            lb1 := l1; ub1 := u1
            lb2 := l2; ub2 := u2
            # allocate storage for my columns
            num_cols : Int := (u2 − l2) div num_procs()
            piece[p] ← Matrix⟨T⟩(l1, u1, 0, num_cols)
        oc
    end
    proc index(i, j : Int)
        if  (j − lb2) mod num_procs() = @ →
            return piece[@][i, (j − lb2) div num_procs()]
        []   else →
            owner : (j − lb2) mod num_procs()
            return piece[owner][i, (j − lb2) div num_procs()]
        fi
    end
    proc assign(i, j : Int, value : T)
        if  (j − lb2) mod num_procs() = @ →
            piece[@][i, (j − lb2) div num_procs()] := value
        []   else →
            owner : (j − lb2) mod num_procs()
            piece[owner][i, (j − lb2) div num_procs()] := value
        fi
    end
end
```

Figure 3.34: The implementation of ScatteredColMatrix

The first step (being odd-numbered) compares and exchanges the first and second elements and also the third and fourth, yielding

$$[\; 2 \quad 4 \quad 1 \quad 3 \;]$$

The second step compares the second and third elements and exchanges them:

$$[\; 2 \quad 1 \quad 4 \quad 3 \;]$$

(The first and last elements have no partners and are therefore not affected.) The third step again compares and exchanges the first and second elements and the third and fourth elements:

$$[\; 1 \quad 2 \quad 3 \quad 4 \;]$$

In this example the array becomes sorted after three steps so the fourth step compares the second and third elements but leaves them in place.

This algorithm can be adapted to MIMD computers by dividing the vector to be sorted into blocks and performing what might be called an odd-even merge sort. For example, consider the array

$$[\; 8 \quad 7 \quad 6 \quad 5 \quad 4 \quad 3 \quad 2 \quad 1 \;]$$

This can be divided into blocks of size two:

$$[\; 8 \quad 7 \; | \; 6 \quad 5 \; | \; 4 \quad 3 \; | \; 2 \quad 1 \;]$$

First the blocks are sorted individually:

$$[\; 7 \quad 8 \; | \; 5 \quad 6 \; | \; 3 \quad 4 \; | \; 1 \quad 2 \;]$$

Then, following the same steps as the odd-even transposition sort, the first and second blocks are merged and split, as are the third and fourth blocks. Merging the first and second blocks yields

$$[\; 5 \quad 6 \quad 7 \quad 8 \;]$$

Similarly, merging the third and fourth blocks yields

$$[\; 1 \quad 2 \quad 3 \quad 4 \;]$$

Then the two blocks are split into blocks of two again, yielding

$$[\; 5 \quad 6 \; | \; 7 \quad 8 \; | \; 1 \quad 2 \; | \; 3 \quad 4 \;]$$

This completes the first step. The second step splits and then merges the second and third blocks, resulting in

$$[\; 5 \quad 6 \; | \; 1 \quad 2 \; | \; 7 \quad 8 \; | \; 3 \quad 4 \;]$$

The third step again splits and merges the first and second block and the third and fourth block:

$$[\; 1 \quad 2 \quad | \quad 5 \quad 6 \quad | \quad 3 \quad 4 \quad | \quad 7 \quad 8 \;]$$

Finally, the second and third block are merged and split, completing the sort. Note that the pattern of merge-split steps follows exactly the pattern of compare-exchange steps in the odd-even transposition sort.

Both sequential sorting and merging exhibit considerable locality of reference since they are done block-wise. This yields an efficient implementation on MIMD computers. Each block is assigned to a processor. In the initial step, each block is sorted. This step is entirely local and the blocks can be sorted in parallel. Then the processors engage in a series of merge-split steps; each corresponds to a compare-exchange step in the original algorithm. Each merge-split step takes place between two processors. If the original compare-exchange steps were independent, the corresponding merge-split steps can be executed in parallel.

There are several ways to accomplish the merge-split step between two processors. The simplest is for the two processors to exchange their blocks. Each then performs a merge of the two blocks; one processor keeps the high elements and discards the low, the other keeps the low elements and discards the high. Figure 3.35 contains an outline of the procedure merge_high, which exchanges blocks with processor partner and merges the two blocks, keeping the high elements. First the local block is sent to partner and partner's block is received. This is done by means of a vector of operations exch. Then the two blocks are merged, discarding the low values. (We use send and receive, instead of assignment, for illustrative purposes; it shows how distributed programming constructs can be used in parallel programs.) The code for merge_low is similar.

Figure 3.36 contains code for the merge-split version of odd-even transposition sort. It follows the algorithm described above. First, the blocks are each sorted using a sequential sorting algorithm. Then n merge-split steps are executed. In alternate steps, the processors merge their blocks with the next higher- or lower-numbered processor. When merging with a higher-numbered processor, they take the smaller elements by executing merge_low; when merging with a lower-numbered processor they take the larger elements by executing merge_high.

Figure 3.37 contains the merge-split version of Batcher's merge-exchange sort. (A good explanation of this algorithm can be found in [70, pages 111-114].) Batcher's algorithm is completely regular and requires

$$\frac{1}{2}\lceil \lg n \rceil \left(\lceil \lg n \rceil + 1 \right)$$

parallel compare-exchange steps to sort n integers.

```
proc merge_high(partner : Int)
    # send my block to "partner"
    send exch[partner](my_block)
    # wait until he has sent his block
    receive exch(his_block)
    # copy my block into temporary
    temp : Vector⟨Int⟩(lb, ub)
    temp := my_block
    # merge "temp" and "his_block" into "my_block,"
    # keeping higher elements
    tptr := ub;  hptr := ub
    fa i := ub downto lb →
        if  tptr ≥ lb and temp[tptr] ≥ his_block[hptr] →
            my_block[i] := temp[tptr]; tptr − −
        []   else my_block[i] := his_block[hptr]; hptr − −
    af
end
```

Figure 3.35: The procedure merge_high

3.6.2 Scheduling and Mapping

Scheduling and mapping are trivial. The shared array is mapped by block to processors, using the resource BlockVector (introduced in Section 1.3).

a : Vector⟨Int⟩(0, n − 1) {use BlockVector}
{map a : block}

Scheduling annotations are unnecessary since the concurrent statement is Figure 3.37 implicitly specifies id_scheduler.

3.6.3 Implementing the Concrete Resource

Figure 3.38 contains the implementation of BlockVector, which is similar to previous implementations of matrices. The internal representation is an IdVector of blocks, along with some private variables to store array bounds. The initial operation, in parallel, saves the bounds of the vector, calculates the size of the local block, and allocate¡s storage for local blocks. The index operation checks to see if the access is local; if so it returns the local value, if not it calculates the owner and returns the remote value. Similarly, the assign operation checks to see if the access is local. If so, it assigns the specified value to an element of the local block; if not, it performs a remote assignment.

```
program odd_even
    n : 10000
    a : Vector⟨Int⟩(0, n − 1) {use BlockVector}
    # operations to exchange blocks, used in
    # "merge_high" and "merge_low".
    exch : Private⟨op(Vector⟨Int⟩)
    # initialize a
    fa  i := 0 to n − 1 → a[i] := random() fa
    # sort individual blocks using sequential sort
    ...
    fa  step := 1 to n →
        co  p := processors →
            if  (p mod 2 = 0) = (step mod 2 = 0) →
                if  p < max_proc() → merge_low(p + 1) fi
            []  else →
                if  p > min_proc() → merge_high(p − 1) fi
            fi
        oc
    af
    proc exchange_high... end
    proc exchange_low ... end
end
```

Figure 3.36: Merge-split version of the odd-even transposition sort.

3.7   Summary

This chapter showed how regular algorithms can be programmed in a portable, efficient, and clear way. Several examples were given. In each case we began with a clear, architecture-independent algorithm, which was annotated to yield an efficient program for MIMD computers:

- We first added scheduling annotations. Since the algorithms in this chapter were regular, we partitioned the chores among the processors statically, assigning roughly an equal number of chores to each processor.

  Scheduling by static partitioning of chores is applicable whenever chore sizes are predictable. This method of scheduling incurs much less overhead than the more general methods described in the next chapter.

- We added mapping annotations to specify data layout. In each example, we specified mappings that make each datum local to the task that uses it. In some

```
program merge_exchange
    n : 10000
    a : Vector⟨Int⟩(0, n − 1) {use BlockVector}
    # operations to exchange blocks, used in
    # "merge_high" and "merge_low".
    exch : Private⟨op(Vector⟨Int⟩)
    # initialize a
    fa i := 0 to n − 1 →  a[i] := random() fa
    # sort individual blocks using sequential sort
    ...
    # tt = largest power of 2 less than n
    tt : Int(1)
    do tt < n →  tt * := 2 od
    tt div := 2
    p = tt
    do p > 0 →
        q := tt
        r := 0
        d := p
        do q ≥ p →
            co p := processors →
                i : Int := p − min_proc()
                if  ixorp = r →  merge_low(p + d)
                []  ixorp − d = r →  merge_high(p − d)
                fi
            oc
            d := q − p
            q div := 2
            r := p
        od
        p div := 2
    od
    proc exchange_high... end
    proc exchange_low ... end
end
```

Figure 3.37: Merge-split adaptation of Batcher's sorting algorithm

```
resource BlockVector⟨T⟩
    extends Vector⟨T⟩
body
    # storage for blocks
    block : IdVector⟨ref⟨Matrix⟨T⟩⟩⟩
    # bounds of vector
    glb, gub : Private⟨Int⟩
    # bounds of local block
    lb, ub : Private⟨Int⟩
    proc initial(l, u)
        co p := processors →
            glb := l; gub := u
            lb, ub := partition(l, u, 1, num_procs(), p − low_proc())
            block[p] ← Vector⟨T⟩(lb, ub)
        oc
    end
    proc index(i : Int)
        if  lb ≤ i and i ≤ ub →
            return block[@][i]
        []  else →
            who : Int := owner(glb, gub, 1, num_procs(), i)
            return block[who][i]
        fi
    end
    proc assign(i : Int, v : T)
        if  lb ≤ i and i ≤ ub →
            block[@][i] := v
        []  else →
            who : Int := owner(glb, gub, 1, num_procs(), i)
            block[who][i] := v
        fi
    end
end
```

Figure 3.38: The implementation of BlockVector

cases, such as matrix addition (Section 3.1), the mappings were partitions that mirrored the scheduler. In the matrix multiplication and region labeling examples (Sections 3.3 and 3.4), the mappings were more complex; some elements of data structures were replicated to improve performance.

The Gaussian elimination example illustrated the interplay between mapping and scheduling. The scheduler used scattered decomposition to achieve load balancing. The requirement that each datum be local to the task that used it dictated the way the data is mapped to processors.

- We annotated declarations of shared objects to specify concrete implementations of the mappings.

- We gave implementations of each concrete resource. The concrete resources were written using generic resources to make them more reusable. The mappings illustrated in this chapter—blocks, strips, columns, etc.— are widely used in programming regular problems on parallel computers [5, 23, 48, 75].

In each example, the architecture-dependent details were separated from the statement of the algorithm; in each example the final program retained the clarity of the original algorithm while also specifying an efficient computation.

Chapter 4

Irregular Problems

This chapter shows how irregular algorithms can be programmed in a portable, efficient, and clear way. By an *irregular* algorithm we mean an algorithm whose flow of control and patterns of access are not predictable. As with regular problems, we begin with a clear, explicitly parallel statement of the algorithm and add annotations for efficiency. The difference is in the design of schedulers and mappings. Since it is impossible to predict the best assignment of chores to processors for an irregular algorithm, schedulers do not specify a particular assignment of chores to processors but instead specify an algorithm to perform the assignment at execution time.

In contrast with Chapter 3, in this chapter there is little emphasis on specifying specific mappings for data structures. In annotating irregular algorithms, instead of specifying a specific storage pattern for a data structure, we instead specify data management policies. These policies adapt to the calculation, often using replication and caching techniques to reduce remote data access.

The rest of this chapter is a series of examples illustrating the Par method applied to irregular problems:

Trapezoidal Integration introduces dynamic schedulers. We relax the restriction of Section 3.2 that the time required to evaluate the function be constant.

Primality Testing I illustrates the use of caching as a strategy for managing distributed data.

Primality Testing II introduces the use of generative communication [50] to build data structures that provide implicit synchronization.

A Parallel Spreadsheet illustrates the use of generative communication to implement distributed data structures.

Adaptive Quadrature illustrates the use of recursive concurrent statements, which often arise in divide-and-conquer algorithms.

4.1 Trapezoidal Integration

```
program trapezoidal
    io : Stdio
    a, b : Real;  n : Int
    io.print("Enter a,b, and n : "); io.read(a, b, n)
    h : (b − a)/n
    result : Real(0.0)
    co i := 0 to n →
        if  i = 0 →  result + := f(a)/2.0
        []  i = n →  result + := f(b)/2.0
        []    else →  result + := f(a + i ∗ h)
        fi
    oc
    result ∗ := h
    io.print("the result is ", result)
    # sample function to integrate
    proc f(x : Real) return sin(x) end
end
```

Figure 4.1: Par program implementing the trapezoidal rule.

Problem: Given a real valued function f of a real parameter, estimate the integral of f over the interval $[a, b]$ by the trapezoidal rule using n sub-intervals:

$$\int_a^b f(x)dx \approx h \left(f(a)/2 + \sum_{i=1}^{n-1} f(a + ih) + f(b)/2 \right)$$

where

$$h = (b − a)/n$$

In Section 3.2 we developed a program for this problem under the assumption that the execution time of f was constant. In this section we drop that restriction; the execution time of f is allowed to vary unpredictably. (For example, the function f could be a Tailor-series polynomial with the number of terms required for convergence varying depending on the value of x.)

The algorithm, repeated from Chapter 3, is shown in Figure 4.1.

4.1.1   Adding Scheduling Annotations

Recall that in Chapter 3 the chores of the concurrent statement were partitioned statically among the available processors so that each processor was responsible for approximately the same number of chores. This strategy works well if all the chores

```
scheduler fcfs(p, lb, ub, s : Int)
    shared op get_task() returns int
    if  p = min_proc() →  # I am the administrator
        # distribute chores
        fa  ch := lb to ub by s →
            in get_task() →  return ch ni
        af
        # distribute stop signals
        fa  i := min_proc() + 1 to max_proc() →
            in get_task() →  return ub + 1 ni
        af
    []  else →  # I am a worker
        t := get_task()
        do t ≤ ub →
            chore(t)
            t := get_task()
        od
    fi
end fcfs
```

Figure 4.2: The fcfs scheduler.

require the same amount of work. However, if the execution time of chores varies widely, this can result a load imbalance between processors and thus an inefficient program. For example, suppose that the function f can be calculated quickly for arguments near a, but that argument values near b result in lengthy computations. Then if the static partitioning strategy of Chapter 3 is used, the processor numbered min_proc will finish long before max_proc and the computation will take longer than necessary.

Since chore execution time cannot be predicted, what is needed is a method of scheduling chores that adapts dynamically to the computation. One such method is based on the administrator-worker paradigm [52]. One processor acts an administrator; it supplies tasks to the other processors on a first-come, first-served basis. The other processors act as workers; they repeatedly acquire a task from the administrator and execute it.

The scheduler fcfs, which implements this strategy, is shown in Figure 4.2. The operation get_task is used for communication between the administrator and workers. It takes no parameters and returns an integer that represents a single chore. (Since get_task is declared to be **shared**, all instances of fcfs will refer to the same operation.) Processor min_proc acts as the administrator. It iterates through the chore numbers, returning each chore number to the first worker that requests it. After all the chores have been distributed, the administrator signals the workers to stop by returning an invalid chore number, ub + 1. The administrator terminates after a stop signal has been returned to each worker.

The processors other than min_proc act as workers. Each repeatedly requests a chore number from the administrator by invoking get_task. If the chore number is ub + 1 the worker terminates; otherwise the worker executes the chore and requests another.

The administrator-worker strategy avoids the problem of load imbalance between processors because if a processor acquires a chore that requires a long time to execute, it simply executes fewer chores. However, if the chores are small, the overhead of acquiring chores one at a time may be excessive, especially on multicomputers, where acquiring a chore requires a remote invocation. The fcfs scheduler can easily be modified so that workers acquire multiple chores per request. As before, the administrator waits for requests and returns chore numbers. Now, however, each chore number a represents the set of chores $\{a, a + s, a + 2s, \ldots, a + (c - 1)s\}$, where c is the number of chores per task. The workers therefore acquire ranges of chores and execute the chores in that range before requesting more work.

Figure 4.3 contains the enhanced version of fcfs. The optional parameter chunk is the number of chores per task. If it not provided it defaults to one, which duplicates the functionality of the original version of fcfs.

Using the enhanced version of fcfs, the concurrent statement of Figure 4.1 can annotated as follows:

```
co i := 0 to n {scheduler fcfs(chunk := 10)} →
    if  i = 0 →  result + := f(a)/2.0
    []  i = n →  result + := f(b)/2.0
    []   else  →  result + := f(a + i * h)
    fi
oc
```

This has the effect of creating tasks of ten chores each and scheduling these tasks on a first come, first served basis. The chunk size can easily be modified to tailor the program to a different computer.

4.1.2   Adding Implementation Annotations

The only shared data structure in this program is result, which is used as an accumulator. Thus, as in Section 3.2, the declaration of result is annotated to use the concrete resource AccRealSum:

result : Real {use AccRealSum}

```
scheduler fcfs(p, lb, ub, s : Int, optional chunk : Int(1))
    shared op get_task() returns int
    if  p = min_proc() → # I am the administrator
        # distribute chores
        fa  ch := lb to ub by s * chunk →
            in get_task() →  return ch ni
        af
        # distribute stop signals
        fa  i := min_proc() + 1 to max_proc() →
            in get_task() →  return ub + 1 ni
        af
    []  else →  # I am a worker
        t := get_task()
        do t ≤ ub →
            fa  ch := t to min(ub, t + s * (chunk − 1)) by s →
                chore(ch)
            af
            t := get_task()
        od
    fi
end
```

Figure 4.3: Enhanced version of the fcfs scheduler.

4.2 Primality Testing

This section illustrates the use of caching, which is a valuable technique for limiting the number of non-local references. It is especially useful in cases such as the following, where items are written once (or only a few times) and read many times.

Problem: Given an integer n, test the integers $1 \ldots n$ for primality. Each integer i is tested for primality by checking for divisibility by primes less than or equal to $\sqrt{i}$.

4.2.1 Algorithm

This problem was suggested in [34] as a good example for exploring parallel programming techniques. The issue that makes this problem interesting is that primality of an integer i is defined in terms of smaller primes; the primality of i cannot be computed before the primality of all the integers $2, \ldots, \sqrt{i}$ has been determined. This suggests the algorithm shown in Figure 4.4. First the upper limit, n, is read and a vector of

```
program prime
   io : Stdio
   n : Int := read_int("Enter maximum:  ")
   prime : Vector⟨Bool⟩(2, n)
   prime[2] := true
   top : Int := 2
   do top < n →
      new_top := min(top * top, n)
      co i := top + 1 to new_top →
         prime[i] := is_prime(i)
      oc
      top := new_top
   od
   fa i := 2 to n →
      if  prime[i] →  io.print(i)
   af
   proc is_prime(i : Int)
      fa  t := 2 to floor(sqrt(i)) →
         if  prime[t] and (i mod t = 0) →  return false fi
      af
      return true
   end
end
```

Figure 4.4: Primality testing

the proper size is declared. To start the process, prime[2] is set to true. The variable top records the largest number that has been checked for primality; thus it also is initially set to 2. The algorithm then iteratively calculates the primality of increasing ranges of integers; in each iteration the maximum number to be checked for primality is squared. First 3 and 4 are checked (concurrently) for primality, then $5 \ldots 16$, $17 \ldots 256$, $257 \ldots 256^2$, and so forth until n is reached. This algorithm guarantees that the primality of each integer i is computed only after the primality of all the integers $2 \leq i \leq \sqrt{i}$ have been computed. Notice that after the first few iterations this algorithm exhibits a high degree of parallelism.

4.2.2   Adding Scheduling Annotations

The amount of calculation needed to determine primality is highly variable; thus an adaptive scheduler such as the scheduler fcfs described in section 4.1.1 is appropriate.

Annotated, the concurrent statement in Figure 4.4 would appear as follows for a chunk size of 1000:

```
co i := top + 1 to new_top {scheduler fcfs(chunk := 1000)} →
    prime[i] := is_prime(i)
oc
```

Of course, the optimal size for chunk depends on n, the number of processors, and other factors.

4.2.3 Adding Implementation Annotations

The only shared data structure used in this program is the vector prime. On NUMA and distributed computers, a naive implementation of Vector would perform poorly since many remote references would be necessary. However, prime is used in a rather specialized way that allows a more efficient implementation. Each element of prime is written exactly once. Some elements, the lower numbered ones, are read by all the processors. However, most elements—those greater than $\sqrt{n}$—are read only once (when they are printed). Also, with the scheduler specified in the previous section, access to prime exhibits a high locality of reference; if a processor accesses prime[i] it is likely to access prime[i + 1], prime[i + 2], and so forth.

One way to take advantage of these facts is to partition the vector into blocks and use a caching strategy to manage each block. When a processor attempts to read or write a vector element, the entire block that contains that element is transferred to the processor. Until another processor requests the same block for writing, the original processor can use other elements from the same block without remote access. We call this vector implementation CachedVector; the declaration of prime is thus annotated as follows:

prime : Vector⟨Bool⟩(2, n) {use CachedVector}

The next section contains an implementation of CachedVector.

4.2.4 Implementing a Cached Vector

In this section we give an implementation of CachedVector based on a central server. The central server manages each block of the vector as a separate instance of the readers/writers problem [41]: writers have exclusive access to blocks while readers can share a block with any number of other readers.

The outline of the resource CachedVector is shown in Figure 4.5. The req_read

```
resource CachedVector⟨T⟩
    extends Vector⟨T⟩
end
    # operations to request blocks
    op req_read(bl, reader : Int)
    op req_write(bl, writer : Int)
    # operations to invalidate blocks
    inv_read : IdVector⟨op(bl : Int)⟩
    inv_write : IdVector⟨op(bl : Int) returns Vector⟨T⟩⟩
    process central_server({on min_proc()})...
    process invalidate_server(p := min_proc() to max_proc(){on p})...
    proc index(i : Int)...
    proc assign(i : Int, v : T)...
    proc initial(l, u : Int, chunk : Int := 100)...
end
```

Figure 4.5: Outline of the resource CachedVector.

---

and req_write operations are used to request read-only or writable blocks from the central server. The operation vectors inv_read and inv_write are used by the central server to invalidate cached copies of blocks. We first describe the processes central_server and invalidate_server, which implement the cache-management strategy. (The **on** clause in the heading of central_server causes it to be executed on min_proc; similarly, the **on** clause in the heading of invalidate_server causes an instance of that server to be executed on each processor min_proc ... max_proc.) Then we describe the implementation of the standard vector operations index, assign, and initial.

The central server.   The central_server process manages the blocks of the vector. Its purpose it to provide clients with access to blocks while maintaining the normal semantics of a vector. To accomplish this, the server ensures that the number of writable copies of a block never exceeds one and that if a writable copy of a block is extant there are no read-only copies.

The central server keeps information about the blocks in a vector of records declared as follows:

```
record Block
    reader : List⟨Int⟩
    writer : Int
    data : ref⟨Vector⟨T⟩⟩
end
block : ref⟨Vector⟨Block⟨T⟩⟩⟩
```

For each block, the server maintains a list of readers, a writer (if there is one) and the master copy of the data in the block. The master copy may temporarily contain invalid data if a writable copy of the block exists. The vector block contains one element for each block in the vector.

Figure 4.6 contains code for the central server. This process consists of a single infinite loop containing an input statement. The input statement services two operations: req_read and req_write. The operation req_read handles requests for read-only copies of a specified block. The code for req_read first checks to see if any processor has a writable copy of the block. If so, the writable copy is retrieved and assigned to the master copy. This is done by invoking the inv_write operation of the current writer. Then the identity of the client is recorded in the readers list of the block and a copy of the block is returned to the reader. (The list manipulation operations are explained in Section 2.6.)

The operation req_write is similar. If there is a writer, the block is retrieved and assigned to the master copy. This is done by invoking the inv_write operation of the current writer. If there are read-only copies of blocks, they are invalidated by invoking the inv_read operation of each reader. Finally, the identity of the writer is recorded and a copy of the master block is returned to the client.

Invalidation servers. Each processor keeps a list of blocks of which it currently has copies. It also keeps track of whether each block is read-only or writable. The data structures required for this are as follows:

```
record LocalBlock
    bn : Int
    writable : Bool
    data : ref⟨Vector⟨T⟩⟩
end
myblocks : Private⟨List⟨LocalBlock⟩⟩
```

The field bn is the block number, writable indicates whether the block is writable, and data contains the actual contents of the block. One each processor, the list myblocks is a list of cached blocks.

```
process central_server()
   record Block... end
   block : ref⟨Vector⟨Block⟨T⟩⟩⟩
   do true →
      in req_read(bl, id : Int) →
         # if there is a writer, get the block back
         if  block[bl].writer ≥ min_proc() →
             block[bl].data := inv_write[block[bl].writer](bl)
             block[bl].writer := min_proc() − 1
         fi
         # record reader and return copy of block
         block[bl].readers.put(id)
         return block[bl].data
      []  req_write(bl, id : Int) →
         # if there is a writer, get the block back
         if  block[bl].writer ≥ min_proc() →
             block[bl].data := inv_write[block[bl].writer](bl)
         # if there are readers, invalidate their blocks
         []  not block[bl].readers.empty() →
             block[bl].readers.to_left()
             do block[bl].readers.right() →
                inv_read[block[bl].readers.value()](bl)
                block[bl].readers.delete()
             od
         fi
         # record writer and return copy of block
         block[bl].writer := id
         return block[bl].data
      ni
   od
end central_server
```

Figure 4.6: Central server for CachedVector

Recall that the central server invalidates read-only blocks when a writable copy is requested, and invalidates writable blocks when any copy is requested. Each processor has a special process that handles requests from the server to invalidate blocks. Invalidating a read-only block is done by simply eliminating it from the local list. Invalidating a writable block requires sending it back to the server.

Figure 4.7 contains code for the invalidation server that runs on each processor. The operation inv_read invalidates read-only blocks. It does this by searching the block list for bl and deleting that block. The operation inv_write invalidates writable blocks. It is similar to inv_read except that the invalidated block is returned to the central server after being removed from the local block list.

Access functions. Access to vector elements is through the procedures index and assign. To decrease overhead in the typical case, each processor keeps track of the most-recently used block separately from the other cached blocks. The declarations required are as follows:

> mru : Private⟨**ref**⟨Vector⟨T⟩⟩⟩
> mru_lb, mru_ub : Private⟨Int⟩
> mru_writable : Private⟨Bool⟩

The variable mru is a reference to the data, mru_lb and mru_ub are the bounds of that vector, and mru_writable indicates whether the most-recently-used block is writable.

Figure 4.8 contains code for the index procedure. The procedure index first checks to see if the index falls in the most-recently used block. If it does, the value is returned immediately. Note that in this case—the typical case if the application displays good locality of reference—vector access requires two operations on a local semaphore and a bounds check.

If the index does not fall in the most-recently-used block, the procedure to_front is invoked. Figure 4.9 contains code for this procedure. The first parameter is a block number, the second parameter indicates whether a writable copy is needed. (In the index procedure, a writable block is not necessary.) The procedure to_front searches the local block list for the required block. If the block is found, it is moved to the front of the list. If the block is not cached locally, it is obtained from the central server by invoking req_read and is then prepended to the list. In either case, mru is updated to point to the new block.

Figure 4.10 contains the assign operation. The logic of procedure assign is almost identical to that of index. Since the assign operation modifies an element of the vector, a writable block is required. Again, access to the most-recently-used block requires two local semaphore operations and a bounds check.

Finally, Figure 4.11 contains the initial procedure, which calculates the block size

```
lock : Private⟨Semaphore⟩ # lock for cached block list
process invalidate_server(p := min_proc() to max_proc(){on p})
    do true →
        in  inv_read[p](bl : Int) →
            lock.p()   # lock local list
            # find block and delete it
            myblocks.to_left()
            do myblocks.right() →
                if  myblocks.value().bn = bl →
                    myblocks.delete()
                    exit
                fi
            od
            lock.v()   # unlock local list
        [] inv_write[p](bl : Int) →
            lock.p()   # lock local list
            # find block and delete it
            myblocks.to_left()
            do myblocks.right() →
                if  myblocks.value().bn = bl →
                    temp : LocalBlock := myblocks.value()
                    myblocks.delete()
                    lock.v()   # unlock local list
                    return temp.data
                fi
            od
        ni
    od
end invalidate_server
```

Figure 4.7: Invalidation server for CachedVector

```
proc index(i : Int)
    lock.p()   # lock the local list
    # if it's in "mru," return immediatly
    if  mru_lb ≤ i and i ≤ mru_ub →
        val : T := mru[i]
        lock.v()
        return val
    # otherwise, locate block and set "mru," then return it
    []  else →
        # compute block that "i" resides in
        b : Int := (i − lb) div blocksize
        # move block "b" to front of list
        to_front(b, false)
        # return value after unlocking list
        val : T := mru[i]
        lock.v()
        return val
    fi
end index
```

Figure 4.8: The index procedure for CachedVector

and allocates space for the block list and the master copies of the blocks. Note that CachedVector has an optional parameter chunk which specifies the block size. This can be adjusted to match the block size of the scheduler so that the scheduler and vector work well together.

4.2.5 Summary

With the use of CachedVector, most data access in the program findprimes is local. The resource CachedVector is conceptually simple, although bookkeeping details make it fairly large. The implementation of CachedVector is generic, so it can be used in any application where vectors are used in ways that provide good locality of reference.

4.3   Another Algorithm for Primality Testing

In this section we describe another algorithm for primality testing, based on *generative communication* [50]. In Section 4.2, the order in which the primality of integers is computed is explicitly specified in the control flow of the program. However, the

```
proc to_front(b : Int, writeable : Bool)
    # search local list for " b"
    found : Bool := false
    myblocks.to_left()
    do myblocks.right() →
        if  myblocks.value().bn = b and
                    (not writable or myblocks.value().writable) →
            temp : LocalBlock := myblocks.value()
            myblocks.delete()
            myblocks.to_left; myblocks.put(temp)
            found := true;
            exit
        fi
    od
    # if not in local list, get it from central server
    if   not found →
        new : ref⟨LocalBlock⟩ ← LocalBlock(b, false, req_read(b, @))
        myblocks.to_left(); myblocks.put(new)
    fi
    # set mru to point to first block on list
    myblocks.right()   # move to the first item
    mru ← myblocks.value().data
    mru_lb := myblocks.value().data.lb()
    mru_ub := myblocks.value().data.ub()
    mru_writable := myblocks.value().writable
end
```

Figure 4.9: The procedure to_front

```
proc assign(i : Int, v : T)
    lock.p()    # lock the local list
    if  mru_lb ≤ i and i ≤ mru_ub and mru_writable →
        mru[i] := v
        lock.v()
    []  else →
        # compute block that "i" resides in
        b : Int := (i − lb) div blocksize
        # move block "b" to front of list
        to_front(b, true)
        mru[i] := v
        lock.v()
    fi
end assign
```

Figure 4.10: The assign procedure for CachedVector

```
proc initial(l, u : Int, optional chunk : Int(100))
    # calculate the number of blocks and allocate "block"
    nblocks := (u − l + chunk) div chunk
    block ← Vector⟨Block⟩(0, nblocks − 1)
    # allocate space for master copies of blocks
    fa  i := 1 to nblocks →
        block[i] ← Vector⟨T⟩(l + i * chunk, l + (i + 1) * chunk − 1)
        block[i].writer := min_proc() − 1
    af
    # set "mru" bounds to a null range to indicate no "mru" block
    co p := processors →
        mru_lb := 1
        mru_ub := 0
    oc
end
```

Figure 4.11: The initial procedure for CachedVector

algorithm imposes an order that is stricter than necessary. For example, the computation of the primality of the integers 5 . . . 15 could be started as soon as the primality of 3 has been determined since computing the primality of these integers depends only on the primality of 2 and 3. The algorithm of Section 4.2, however, does not begin to compute the primality of these integers until the primality of 4 has been determined. In the case of primality testing, this does not much matter—there is ample parallelism available anyway. However, in other applications it may be important to utilize every opportunity for parallelism.

A more flexible way to handle complicated synchronization constraints is to use "live data structures" [34] that provide synchronization automatically. A *synchronized bag* is one such data structure.

A synchronized bag has the following specification:

```
resource SynchBag⟨Key, Value⟩
    op put(Key, Value)
    op get(Key) returns Value
    op read(Key) returns Value
end
```

The put operation inserts a (Key, Value) pair in the bag. It is non-blocking. The read operation finds a (Key, Value) pair with a specified key and returns the corresponding value. If no such pair is currently in the bag, the read operation blocks until one is inserted. The get operation is similar to read, but the pair is deleted from the bag before the value is returned.

Figure 4.12 contains a primality testing program that uses a synchronized bag. (This algorithm is adapted from [34].) The main program simply attempts to calculate the primality of all the integers 2 . . . n simultaneously by invoking is_prime on each. After the primality of an integer i has been determined, the pair (i, is_prime(i)) is inserted in the bag. The procedure is_prime determines the primality of k by trial division; each integer td in 2 . . . $\sqrt{k}$ such that td is prime is used as a trial divisor. In the procedure is_prime, the invocation prime.read(td) blocks until the primality of the potential trial divisor td has been inserted in the bag by some other chore. Thus the required synchronization is provided implicitly by a data structure instead of being expressed explicitly in the control flow of the program.

4.3.1   Adding Scheduling Annotations

Again, a dynamic scheduler such as those in Section 4.1.1 is appropriate for this problem since the calculation required to test for primality is unpredictable. Thus we annotate the concurrent statement as follows:

```
program findprimes
   prime : SynchBag⟨Int, Bool⟩
   co i := 2 to n →  prime.put(i, is_prime(i)) oc
   proc is_prime(k)
      lim := floor(sqrt(k))
      fa  td := 2 to lim →
         if  prime.read(td) and (k mod td = 0) →  return false fi
      af
        return true
   end
end findprimes
```

Figure 4.12: Calculating prime numbers.

```
co i := 2 to n {scheduler fcfs(chunk := 1000)} →
   prime.put(i, is_prime(i))
oc
```

Notice that the schedulers of Section 4.1.1 schedule lower-numbered chores first; thus the primality of small integers is checked before larger. This is necessary in this algorithm because scheduling the chores in some other order could result in deadlock.

In general, we insist that schedulers be partially correct. That is, we insist that a correct scheduler terminate only when each chore has been executed exactly once. For efficiency, it is often useful to design schedulers that cannot be guaranteed to terminate in every program. For example, to reduce overhead, it is often useful to execute a collection of chores in some fixed order; sequential execution incurs less overhead than context switching. However, for any fixed execution order, chores can be written that cause deadlock. For example, if a scheduler executes chore(1) before chore(2), deadlock occurs if chore(1) waits for a message from chore(2). Since scheduling each chore as a separate thread is not an efficient alternative, we must allow schedulers that may cause deadlock in some programs.

4.3.2 Implementing a Synchronized Bag

The best way to implement a synchronized bag depends on the architecture of the computer; here we consider implementing a synchronized bag on a multicomputer. Our general strategy is to store each (key, value) pair on one processor, determined by a hash function on the key. The put operation will compute the hash function of key and send a message to the appropriate processor, which will insert the (key, value) pair in a local table. The get and read operations will compute the hash value of key and

```
resource DistSynchBag⟨Key, Value⟩
    op put(Key, Value)
    op read(Key) returns Value
    op get(Key) returns Value
body
    # declare arrays of server ops
    remote_put : IdVector⟨Op(Key, Value)⟩
    remote_read : IdVector⟨Op(Key) returns Value⟩
    remote_get : IdVector⟨Op(Key) returns Value⟩
    proc get(k : Key)...
    proc put(k : Key, v : Value)...
    proc read(k : Key)
    process server(p := min_proc() to max_proc(){on p})...
end DistSynchBag
```

Figure 4.13: Outline of an implementation of DistSynchBag

send a request to the appropriate processor for the corresponding value. If a processor receives a get or read request for a nonexistent key, it delays servicing the request until it receives a put invocation with that key.

The implementation of DistSynchBag uses the resource Table. The specification of Table is as follows:

```
resource Table⟨Key, Value⟩
    op contains(Key) returns Bool # test
    op put(Key, Value)        # insert
    op get(Key) returns Value         # retrieve and delete
    op read(Key) returns Value        # retrieve
end
```

The contains operation returns true if the specified key is in the table. The get, put, and read operations are similar to that of a synchronized bag except that they are all non-blocking. We do not discuss in detail the implementation of Table since it is a standard sequential data structure; it could, for example, be implemented as a hash table or a binary tree.

Figure 4.13 contains an outline of DistSynchBag. Each processor executes one server process that services remote get, put, and read operations. Figure 4.14 contains code for the server. Each server stores (key, value) pairs in a local table. Requests for keys that are not in the table are delayed by the use of a synchronization expression (Section 2.7.2, page 32). The remote_put operation simply inserts the (key, value) pair

```
# service remote requests
process server(p := min_proc() to max_proc() on p)
    t : Table⟨Key, Value⟩ # table to hold local values
    do true →
        in remote_put[p](k, v) →
            t.insert(k, v)
        [] remote_read[p](k) and t.contains(k) →
            return t.value(k)
        [] remote_get[p](k, reply) and t.contains(k) →
            return t.remove(k)
        ni
    od
end
```

Figure 4.14: The server process

in the local table. The remote_get and remote_read operations delay until a pair with the appropriate key has been inserted and then retrieve the associated value.

Figure 4.15 contains the access functions get, put, and read. Each procedure simply calculates the hash function of the key and invokes the corresponding remote operation on the correct processor.

The use of SynchBag in Figure 4.12 is specialized since the get operation is never invoked. This means that once a key enters the bag it is never removed, which permits an important optimization to be made. When a key is requested by read, the value can be cached in a table cached_values on the processor that makes the request. This improvement means that each processor makes only one remote access for each distinct key. Figure 4.16 contains modified versions of the procedures access functions to implement this improvement. Each processor maintains a private table cached_values. The put operation is the same as before. The read operation checks the local table for key before making a remote request; if a remote request is necessary it stores the returned value in the local table. Finally, the get operation issues an error message and aborts the computation.

Thus, in the final version of findprimes, the declaration of primes is annotated as follows:

prime : SynchBag⟨Int, Bool⟩ {use CachedDistSynchBag}

The result is that the primality of each integer is copied exactly once to each processor that needs it.

```
# remove a pair with key "k" and return the corresponding value
proc get(k : Key)
    return remote_get[hash(k)](k)
end
# insert the pair ("k","v") in the bag
proc put(k : Key, v : Value)
    send remote_put[hash(k)](k, v)
end
# return some "v" such that ("k","v") is in the bag
proc read(k : Key)
    return remote_get[hash(k)](k)
end
```

Figure 4.15: Implementation of a synchronized bag: access functions

```
cached_values : Private⟨Table⟨Key, Value⟩⟩
proc put(k : Key, v : Value)
    # insert the pair ("k","v") in the bag ...
    send remote_put[hash(k)](k, v)
end
proc read(k : Key)
    if  cached_values.contains(k) →
        return cached_values.value(k)
    []  else →
        v : Value := remote_get[hash(k)](k)
        cached_values.put(k, v)
        return v
    fi
end
# get is not allowed for cached bags
proc get(k : Key)
    abort("get operation not supported")
end
```

Figure 4.16: A version of **read** with caching.

4.4 A Parallel Spreadsheet

The use of the bag abstraction in the previous example uses a style of communication termed *generative communication* [50]. It is said to be generative because messages, until they are withdrawn, have an independent existence. They are not bound to any particular process or channel; any process can read or remove them. In fact, the process that generates a message may be long extinct before the recipient process is created. (See Section 6.7 for more about generative communication.) The generality of generative communication makes it useful for algorithms that are extremely irregular. In the previous section we used generative communication for purposes of synchronization; in this section we show how generative communication can to implement distributed data structures.

Problem: A spreadsheet is a collection of cells, each of which contains a function that may depend on an arbitrary collection of other cells. The dependence can be very irregular, and the amount of computation required to evaluate the function is unpredictable. Complicated functions, such as

cell[floor(100 * cos(cell[self + 10]))]

can be used so it is impossible to obtain precise dependence information by static analysis. (Functions are represented by strings, which are executed by an interpreter. We will not discuss the implementation of the interpreter.)

A *user* acts upon the data structure described above. The user can modify cell functions in an arbitrary fashion. Each modification of a cell can result in changes to the values of other cells. Given this model, the problem is to attempt to display up-to-date values for each cell in the spreadsheet. After the user modifies a cell, other cells are updated repeatedly until a fixed point is reached (that is, until the values of all the cells become stable). (It is, of course, possible to program nonterminating spreadsheet calculations, which never reach a fixed point. Various rules could be used to deal with this possibility; we have chosen the simplest rule: recalculate forever, or until the user intervenes.) The order in which cells are updated is not specified.

One way to implement a spreadsheet is as a synchronized bag of cells. Figure 4.17 is the skeleton of a spreadsheet program. The cells of the spreadsheet are represented by (index, contents) pairs in a bag. The contents of each cell is a structure containing the fields function and value. The function field is a string to be interpreted; value is the current value of the field. There are three main tasks to accomplish: updating the spreadsheet, handling user input, and displaying the spreadsheet. A separate processes is devoted to each of these activities. Semaphores are used to synchronize the three processes.

Figure 4.18 contains code to update the spreadsheet. The update process is an in-

```
program spreadsheet
  size : Int := 10000   # for example
  record Cell
      function : String
      value : Real
  end
  sc : SynchBag⟨Int, Cell⟩ {use DistSynchBag}
  calculate, display : Semaphore
  # perform initial display
  display.v()
  co  → # update spreadsheet; see Figure 4.18
  //  → # handle user input; see Figure 4.19
  //  → # display spreadsheet; see Figure 4.20
  oc
  proc evaluate(todo : Cell)
      # interpret "todo.function," accessing other
      # cells as necessary by invoking "sc.read"("n")
  end
end spreadsheet
```

Figure 4.17: A spreadsheet evaluator.

---

finite loop. Each iteration calculates a new value for each cell in the spreadsheet. This is done in parallel. Each cell is read, recalculated, and replaced by a new cell if its value changes. If the value of any cell changes during an iteration, a fixed point has not yet been reached and the calculate semaphore is used to signal another recalculation. When a fixed point is reached, the display semaphore is used to signal that the spreadsheet should be redisplayed.

The boolean variable changed is used as an accumulator; therefore its declaration has been annotated to use AccOr (Section 3.4.5). The concurrent statement is annotated to use the fcfs scheduler since the chore size is unpredictable. (Recall that the fcfs scheduler, given in Section 4.1.1, provides dynamic load balancing.)

Figure 4.19 contains an outline of the code to handle user input. After a cell has been edited by the user, the need for a recalculation is signaled. Handling user input is done by getting a cell number from the user (by key-stroke or mouse), removing that cell, editing it, and replacing it. Notice that editing a cell removes the cell from the bag. The effect is that any recalculation that is in progress will block until the editing is complete. This is a useful feature if the user has inadvertently introduced a circular dependency and is trying to remove it.

Figure 4.20 contains code to display the spreadsheet. The code waits for a signal

```
# update spreadsheet; see Figure 4.18
do true →
    calculate.p()    # wait for signal to recalculate
    # update each cell once
    changed : Bool(false) {use AccOr}
    co c := 1 to size {scheduler fcfs} →
        cur : Cell  := sc.read(c)
        new_val : Real := evaluate(cur.function)
        if  new_val ≠ cur.value →
            changed or := true
            sc.get(c)
            sc.put(c, Cell(cur.function, new_val))
        fi
    oc
    # either recalculate or display results
    if  changed → calculate.v()
    []   else → display.v()
    fi
od
```

Figure 4.18: Updating the spreadsheet

```
# handle user input; see Figure 4.19
do true →
    # get a cell number "cn" from the user
    c : Cell := sc.get(cn) # take the cell out of the bag
    # edit "c"
    sc.put(cn, c) # put the cell back
    calculate.v() # signal a recalculation
od
```

Figure 4.19: Handling user input

```
# display spreadsheet; see Figure 4.20
do true →
    display.p() # await a change
    fa  c := 0 to size − 1 →
        val : Value := sc.read(c)
        show(c, val.value)
    af
od
```

Figure 4.20: Displaying the spreadsheet

---

to redisplay and then iterates through the cells, reading and displaying each one. The display loop will block if a cell is being edited by the user.

4.5 Adaptive Quadrature

This section illustrates the use of recursive concurrent statements, which arise naturally in divide-and-conquer algorithms. The use of recursive parallelism requires a different kind of scheduler than those that have been seen thus far.

Problem: Given a real-valued function f on an interval $[a, b]$, find an approximate value for the definite integral

$$\int_a^b f(x)\, dx$$

using adaptive quadrature.

In previous examples, integrals were estimated using the trapezoidal rule, which partitions the interval of integration into n subintervals and evaluates the function at the endpoints of the subintervals. The problem with this approach is that it is difficult to predict how large n must be for a given function f. Functions that vary rapidly require a much finer partition than relatively smooth functions. Moreover, a function may vary rapidly on some parts of $[a, b]$ and be relatively smooth on others; if subintervals of equal size are used throughout the interval, this will result in many more function evaluations than are necessary for a given degree of precision.

The technique of *adaptive quadrature* avoids this problem by partitioning the interval more intelligently. The idea, in its simplest form, is to calculate an approximation to the entire interval using one method; then re-approximate with a more accurate method. If the two approximations match to a specified tolerance, the latter approximation is taken to be the answer. If not, each of two subintervals of the original interval is recursively approximated using the same method. The areas of the two subintervals

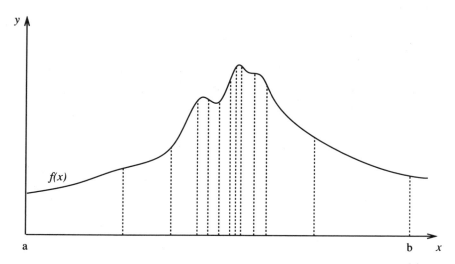

Figure 4.21: Approximating an integral by adaptive quadrature.

can calculated concurrently. (Often the initial number of intervals is chosen to be larger than one, but the principle remains the same.) The partition induced by such a strategy might be similar to that shown in Figure 4.21. Notice that the interval is finely partitioned in regions where f is jagged and coarsely partitioned where f is smooth.

4.5.1 Algorithm

Figure 4.22 contains an unannotated procedure for adaptive quadrature. In this case the area of each segment is approximated by the trapezoidal rule and then by Simpson's rule. (For smooth functions, Simpson's rule provides a more accurate estimate of the integral than the trapezoidal rule.) The concurrency arises because the two recursive calls to area can be executed simultaneously. (For simplicity, this procedure has been written in a way that may cause f(x) to be recalculated many times for each x. This can easily be avoided by passing f(a) and f(b) as parameters, along with a and b, but for our purposes this needlessly complicates the program.)

4.5.2 Adding Scheduling Annotations

This problem has features that require a quite different kind of scheduling strategy than previous problems. In previous examples in this chapter, all the chores to be scheduled arose from the execution of a single concurrent statement. Although chores had unpredictable execution times, the flow of control was predictable; all chores—and thus all schedulers—were created simultaneously. This made it possible for schedulers (such

```
proc area(f : ref⟨op(Real) returns Real⟩, a, b : Real)
    est1 : Real := trapezoidal(f, a, b)
    est2 : Real := simpsons(f, a, b)
    if  close(est1, est2) →
        return est2
    []  else →
        left, right : Real
        co  →
            left := area(f, a, (a + b)/2.0)
        //  →
            right := area(f, (a + b)/2.0, b)
        oc
        return left + right
    fi
end
```

Figure 4.22: Adaptive Quadrature

as fcfs) to cooperate directly in assigning tasks to processors. On the other hand, with nested concurrent statements the situation is more unpredictable. There will be a large and unpredictable collection of tasks that will arise from different invocations of the concurrent statement. At the top level of recursion, the tasks must be scheduled based on imperfect knowledge; there is no way to predict which tasks will generate many sub-tasks and which will terminate quickly. Deeper in the recursion, tasks must be assigned to balance the load across processors.

What is needed is a way to allow instances of a scheduler to cooperate in assigning chores to processors in spite of the fact that the instances are created and destroyed at unpredictable times. One way to accomplish this is to provide an intermediary between instances of scheduler. The intermediary can be represented by an operation which takes no parameters and returns a processor number; for example:

op pick() **returns** Int

The intermediary could use any of several strategies. For example, it could return processor numbers in round-robin order or return a random processor number. Given a large number of tasks, either strategy would tend to balance the load among processors. (For arbitrary distributions of task execution times, the expected speedup of random scheduling tends to the expected speedup of an optimal schedule as the number of tasks approaches infinity [44].) A more elaborate version of pick could keep track of the number of tasks on each processor and return the number of the most lightly loaded processor. This idea is especially attractive if the operating system already provides a system call to determine processor load averages; the pick procedure then becomes a wrapper for this system call.

Using pick, the concurrent statement of Figure 4.22 can be annotated as follows:

```
co {on pick()} →
    left := area(f, a, (a + b)/2.0)
// {on pick()} →
    right := area(f, (a + b)/2.0, b)
oc
```

Since this kind of scheduling is so simple, one might be tempted to use it for all scheduling problems. Indeed, many languages that provide automatic scheduling use schedulers akin to those described above. For completely irregular problems, such schedulers work well. However, such schedulers cannot take advantage of the regularity exhibited by many algorithms; thus they incur more multiprogramming and communication overhead than more specialized schedulers.

In general, the techniques used for irregular problems are simpler and more general (and hence more reusable) than techniques used for regular problems. This outcome is somewhat counterintuitive; we might expect that more complicated and problem-specific techniques would be required to program irregular algorithms efficiently. However, the unpredictability of irregular algorithms makes problem-specific scheduling and mapping techniques difficult to devise. Complex schedulers are needed to take advantage of special properties of an algorithm; an irregular algorithm is, by definition, unpredictable and thus has no special properties—at least, none that can be predicted and taken advantage of.

4.6 Summary

This chapter showed how irregular algorithms can be expressed in a portable, efficient, and clear way. As in chapter 3, we presented several examples, each of which began with a clear, architecture-independent algorithm, which was then annotated to yield an efficient program for MIMD computers:

- We first added scheduling annotations. The examples in this chapter were irregular, making a static assignment of chores to processors inappropriate. Thus dynamic schedulers were specified. In the first four examples, the chores had unpredictable execution times but the flow of control was predictable. In such cases the instances of a scheduler could cooperate directly in assigning chores to processors. We gave two implementations of the scheduler fcfs, which schedules chores dynamically by direct cooperation between instances of the scheduler.

In the last example (Section 4.5), even the flow of control was unpredictable; thus we used an intermediary to facilitate cooperation between instances of the scheduler. We discussed several techniques for programming such schedulers.

- We annotated declarations of shared objects to specify concrete implementations of abstract resources. Section 4.2 illustrated the use of caching to reduce the amount of remote data access. A generic implementation of a cached vector (Section 4.2.4) was given.

  In Section 4.3, we illustrated how generative communication can be used to deal with complicated synchronization constraints. A reusable implementation of a cached, synchronized bag was given. In Section 4.4, generative communication was again used, this time to implement a distributed data structure.

- We gave implementations of each concrete resource. The concrete resources were written generically to make them more widely reusable.

In each example, the architecture-dependent details were separated from the statement of the algorithm; in each example the final program retained the clarity of the original algorithm while also specifying an efficient computation.

Chapter 5

Implementing Par

Par has not yet been implemented, but it has been designed to permit a straightforward implementation. This chapter describes the design of a Par compiler that would generate code for various kinds of MIMD computers: UMA, NUMA, and multicomputers. It should be useful not only as a guide to implementing Par, but as a guide to implementing Par's facilities in other languages.

This chapter is organized as follows. First we present an overview of the way Par programs are executed. The emphasis is on the structure of calculations rather than the compilation process. Then we present, in detail, a design for a Par compiler. Each phase of the compiler is described. Finally, we present an example illustrating the compilation process.

5.1   Overview

Par's compilation units are the program and the resource.   Except for a few syntactic differences, programs are treated as resources that export no operations; thus, in this chapter, when we say "resource" we mean "program or resource." The compiler produces a sequential program for each processor in the computer. The sequential programs invoke run-time support routines to communicate and synchronize.

Generic resources are compiled separately for each set of actual generic parameters. For example, if a program sample uses a List of integers and a list of reals, the following steps would be necessary to compile the program:

```
par List<Int>
par List<Real>
par sample
```

(Here we assume that *par* is the name of the Par compiler.) This may seem to be a large burden to place on the programmer, but we anticipate constructing tools to build configuration-control files for tools such as make [46]. This can be done by automatically extracting resource names and generic parameters from compilation units. The srm utility [91], which performs a similar role for the SR compiler, demonstrates the practicality of this approach.

program blocks

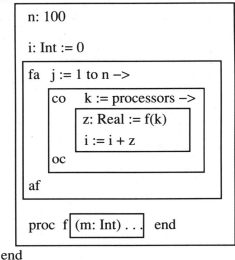

end

Figure 5.1: Block structure of a simple program.

5.1.1   Structure of Programs

Viewed statically, a Par program consists of a collection of blocks. Each block can contain declarations, code, and sub-blocks. Figure 5.1 shows the block structure of a short program. Compound statements, procedures, and processes each form their own block. Blocks are lexically scoped; code in a block can reference data in surrounding blocks. For example, in the body of the concurrent statement in Figure 5.1, the identifiers z, k, j, i, and n are all visible.

5.1.2   Structure of Calculations

The block structure of a program is static. However, the run-time structure of a calculation is dynamic. During a calculation, instances of a block are created and destroyed. Moreover, multiple instances of a block can exist simultaneously. In the example above, num_procs copies of the body of the concurrent statement will be created and then destroyed. These instances can share code, because code is immutable, but each must store its data separately. The data that represents a run-time instance of a block is called an *environment*.

Execution of a Par program begins with a single thread executing on some processor, which we call the *main* processor. This thread begins by allocating an environment

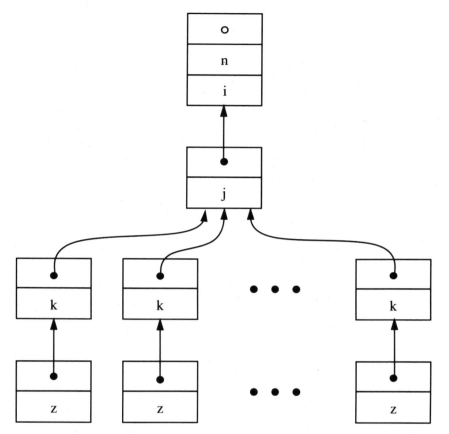

Figure 5.2: Environment structure of the hello program.

for the outermost block. Then it begins to execute the sequential code at the outermost level of the program. Other threads are created by allocating memory for the thread's environment, initializing the environment, and calling a run-time support routine to make the thread runnable.

During the calculation, each processor keeps a reference to the current environment in a well known place such as a processor register. Data in the local block are accessed by applying fixed offsets to the current environment pointer. However, variables in surrounding blocks must also be accessible. This is accomplished by storing in each environment a reference to its lexically containing environment. This is called the *parent pointer*. Figure 5.2 shows a snapshot of the environment structure of program *blocks* after the declaration of z in the concurrent statement. All instances of the concurrent statement share the same instance of the variables n, i, and j but keep

```
process mem_server()
    do true →
        in  read(addr, size : Int) →
        return memory[addr : addr + size − 1]
        []   write(addr, size : Int, value : Vector⟨Byte⟩)
                memory[addr, addr + size − 1] := value
        []   read_id(offset, size : Int) →
                return id_block[offset : offset + size − 1]
        []   write_id(offset, size : Int, value : Vector⟨Byte⟩) →
                id_block[offset : offset + size − 1] := value
        ni
    od
end
```

Figure 5.3: Structure of the memory server on multicomputers.

separate instances of the variables k and z. Arrows represent parent pointers.

Threads access nonlocal variables by following some chain of parent pointers to the variable's environment. (However, much of this indirection can be avoided; see below.) On shared-memory computers, the parent pointer is an address; accessing objects in outer environments is accomplished by one or more levels of indirect addressing. On multicomputers, the parent environment can be on another processor; thus the parent pointer is implemented as a pair (processor, address) where processor is the owner of the parent environment and address is the address of the environment on that processor. In this case, access to an object in the parent environment is accomplished by sending a request to the owner of the parent environment, passing the address of the object and its size. The address is obtained by adding the address of the parent environment to the object's offset within that environment.

On multicomputers, each processor executes a *memory server* process to provide remote data access. (The use of mapping annotations can reduce or eliminate the need for this server, but Par must be able to execute programs that access nonlocal data.) The general structure of the server is shown in Figure 5.3. The array memory is an array of bytes that represents all local memory. The read operation returns a copy of a block of memory; the write operation modifies a block of memory. The operations read_id and write_id are used to access IdVector elements; their use is explained in Section 5.1.3. (This implementation of mem_server assumes that the computer is homogeneous—that all processors have identical data formats. If the computer is not homogeneous, mem_server must also translate data into the proper format.)

Access to nonlocal environments is more expensive than access to the local environment. On shared-memory computers, one or more levels of indirect addressing is required; on multicomputers, message passing may be necessary. Thus it is important to minimize access to nonlocal environments. Several optimizations help in this regard. First, environments can often be merged. For example, in Figure 5.2, the environment that contains j can be merged with the environment that contains n and i. This is possible because (a) they are on the same processor and (b) at most one copy of j exists for each copy of n and i. The environments that contain k and z on each processor can be similarly merged. In general, a collection of environments that corresponds to nested blocks of sequential code satisfies conditions (a) and (b) above, and can always be merged into a single environment.

Another way to reduce access to nonlocal environments is to replicate immutable data in sub-environments. This is especially useful if the sub-environment is on a different processor. In Figure 5.2, for example, the integer n and all the parent pointers are immutable; each could be replicated in all sub-environments. As mentioned earlier (Section 2.10.1), constants do not require mapping because they are replicated wherever they are needed; this is the mechanism by which replication is accomplished.

When a procedure is invoked, synchronously or asynchronously, a new environment is built. The parent pointer for this environment refers to the procedure's lexically enclosing environment. With one exception (explained below), procedures are defined at the outermost level of a program or resource so the parent pointer for a procedure environment refers to environment of the resource or program in which the procedure is defined.

When a concurrent statement with a scheduler is compiled, the body of the concurrent statement is encapsulated in a procedure. (This procedure is invoked when a **chore** statement is executed.) The parent pointer for this procedure refers to the environment of the concurrent statement, not the resource or program environment. Section 5.2.2 describes in more detail how concurrent statements are implemented.

5.1.3 Representing Data

Representations. A representation is a low-level object that is directly supported by the processor architecture. Thus representations are implemented as memory cells in some environment. A representation is allocated on the processor on which the declaration is executed.

Records. A record is implemented by concatenating the data that represents its fields. Recall that the only operations allowed on records are field extraction and element-wise initialization, assignment, and comparison. Since field sizes are fixed and determined at compile-time, any field in a record can be located by applying a fixed offset to the address of the record.

Resources.   We associate with each resource R a record type Env_R that contains the resource environment—the top-level declarations in the body of the resource. We use an instance of Env_R to store the state of each instance of R. For example, in the resource IntStack of Figure 2.4 (page 19), the top level declarations are as follows:

> **body**
>   data : **ref**⟨Vector⟨Int⟩⟩
>   ptr : Int := 1
>   size : Int := 100
>   ...
> **end**

Thus Env_IntStack is defined as

> **record** Env_IntStack
>   data : **ref**⟨Vector⟨Int⟩⟩
>   ptr : Int
>   size : Int
> **end**

Each instance of IntStack will be represented by an instance of Env_Intstack.

IdVectors.   Each processor maintains a block of memory, called the Id-block, that is used to store IdVector elements. An IdVector with base-type B is represented by one instance of B in each Id-block. Each instance of B has the same offset within the Id-block on all processors. As a consequence, the offset of an IdVector serves as a unique identifier for the IdVector. Since the offset of an IdVector is immutable, it can be replicated in sub-environments.

Access to the local element of an IdVector is done by applying a fixed offset to the local Id-block. Access to nonlocal elements is accomplished by sending a message to the memory server on the processor that owns the element. The offset of the nonlocal element (which is the same as the offset of the local element) is passed as a parameter. The memory server described in Section 5.1.2 (page 120) services these requests.

The question remains of how offsets are assigned to instances of IdVector. Since IdVectors can be created and destroyed dynamically, the compiler cannot assign offsets statically; instead, a central server is used. The central server resides on the main processor—the processor that executes the initial program thread. Allocating an Id-Vector offset is accomplished by invoking the run-time support routine id_offset with the size of the base type. The return value is the offset. The Id-block is managed in the same way as is free store in traditional, imperative languages such as C or Pascal. For IdVectors that are created in the main thread, allocating an offset is a local operation and will be no more expensive than dynamic allocation in sequential languages. This is the usual case, since IdVectors are usually used to represent shared, distributed data structures, and thus are declared outside concurrent statements. (In Chapters 3 and 4, all declarations of IdVectors were in the main thread.)

References. References to representations and records are implemented as pointers. On a shared-memory computer, a pointer is an address; on a multicomputer, a pointer is a (machine, address) pair.

References to resources are somewhat more complicated. A reference to a resource instance is a tuple $(e, o_1, \ldots, o_n)$. The pointer e is the environment pointer—the address of the data associated with the resource instance. This pointer is used as the parent pointer for all invocations of resource operations. Each o_i, for $1 \le i \le n$, is the information needed to invoke the ith exported operation. If the ith operation is implemented by a procedure, o_i is the address of that procedure. (Note that references to procedures are always local addresses, even on multicomputers. This is because identical code is loaded on all processors of a multicomputer; thus the address of a procedure is independent of the processor.) If the ith operation is implemented by an input statement, o_i is a pointer to a queue where that operation's messages are stored. This pointer is a (processor, address) pair on a multicomputer. Section 5.2.4 describes how queues are used to implement input statements.

A reference to an operation is implemented in the same way as a reference to a resource with one operation; that is, as a (processor, pointer) pair.

A reference to an IdVector is represented by the offset of the IdVector within the Id-block.

5.2 Compiling Par Programs

The proposed Par compiler consistes of several phases:

- The *parser* accepts Par programs and resources as input and emits an abstract syntax tree that represents the entire program or resource. Subsequent compiler phases operate on this parse tree.

- The *concurrent* phase rewrites concurrent statements into a canonical form. First, concurrent statements with multiple arms are translated to nested concurrent statements, each with one arm. Then concurrent statements that use schedulers other than id_scheduler are transformed into concurrent statements that use only id_scheduler.

- The *input* phase translates input statements into calls to the run-time support.

- The *expression* phase transforms operators into invocations, according to **overload** declarations.

- The *type* phase assigns types to nodes in the parse tree that represent values. It also substitutes concrete types (as specified in implementation clauses) for abstract types.

- The *invocation* phase expands operation invocations into simple procedure calls.

- The *elaborate* phase elaborates declarations.

- Finally, various code generators produce code for particular architectures.

The *invocation* and *elaborate* phases invoke each other recursively. This is because expanding an invocation can result in additional declarations, while elaborating a declaration may produce additional invocations. All but the last phase are common to the various architectures.

The next section discusses how data is represented in Par calculations. Subsequent sections describe each phase of the compiler in turn. In the final section we present an example of how the phases would work in practice.

5.2.1   Parsing Par Programs

Lexical analysis of Par programs is straightforward. The Par language contains no constructs that cannot be handled by standard scanner-generators such as Lex. A Lex-compatible scanner has been written for Par.

A parser for Par has been written using the YACC parser generator. The parser produces an abstract syntax tree, which is used by subsequent stages of the compiler. Figure 5.4 contains a small example, the syntax tree for the following trivial program:

```
program donothing
    foo : Int
    foo := 3 + 4
end
```

The syntax tree is a convenient representation for program transformations.

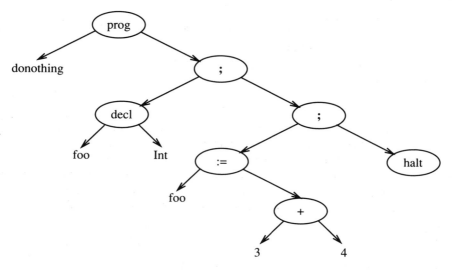

Figure 5.4: A syntax tree.

5.2.2 Simplifying Concurrent Statements

This section describes how concurrent statements are simplified. The goal of concurrent statement simplification is to reduce all concurrent statements to a canonical form. Concurrent statements with multiple arms are translated to equivalent statements with only one arm, and all concurrent statements are rewritten to use either no scheduler or the built-in id_scheduler. In this form, the implementation of concurrent statements can be encapsulated in a single run-time support routine, which is described on page 127.

Concurrent statments with multiple arms are translated into nested concurrent statements. For example,

```
co i := 1 to N  →  cobody1
//      →  cobody2
//  j := 1 to M  →  cobody3
oc
```

is translated to

```
co arm := 0 to 2 →
    if  arm = 0 →  co i := 1 to N →  cobody1 oc
    []  arm = 1 →  cobody2
    []  arm = 2 →  co j := 1 to N →  cobody3 oc
    fi
oc
```

(Of course, the translation is actually done on the syntax tree, not on the program text.) The outer concurrent statement will be executed by forking three threads on the current processor since a concurrent statement without a scheduler specifies multiprogramming, not true parallelism. Two of these threads will fork again almost immediately.

Next, we transform concurrent statements with schedulers so that they use only id_scheduler. A concurrent statement annotated with the scheduler forall is simply changed to a for-all statement with the same quantifier and body. For example, the concurrent statement

$$\textbf{co } i := a \textbf{ to } b \textbf{ \{scheduler } forall\} \rightarrow \textbf{ cobody oc}$$

is translated to

$$\textbf{fa } i := a \textbf{ to } b \rightarrow \textbf{ cobody af}$$

The same transformation applies if there are multiple quantifiers.

A concurrent statement with a scheduler that is neither id_scheduler nor forall is translated into a scheduler that uses id_scheduler. (The id_scheduler is simple to implement since it specifies exactly one thread per processor.) The body of the concurrent statement is translated into a procedure with one parameter for each quantifier variable. For example,

$$\textbf{co } i := a \textbf{ to } b \textbf{ by } c \textbf{ \{scheduler } name\} \rightarrow \text{...oc}$$

is transformed into the following:

```
co p := min_proc() to max_proc() {scheduler id_scheduler} →
    name(cobody, a, b, c)
oc
```

This statement will be implemented by forking one thread on each processor. Each thread executes the scheduler *name*; when all instances of the scheduler have terminated the concurrent statement terminates.

Above, cobody is a reference to a procedure that encapsulates the body of the concurrent statement:

```
proc cobody(i : Int)
    ...
end
```

Recall (Section 2.10.2) that the instances of scheduler name are collectively responsible for executing a **chore** statement once for each value of the quantifier variable i. The **chore** statement is implemented by invoking cobody with appropriate parameters.

A concurrent statement with both a scheduler and an **on** statement is translated similarly. For example,

```
co lb to ub by step {scheduler name on lb to ub} → ...oc
```

is translated to

```
co p := lb to ub {scheduler id_scheduler} →
    name(cobody, a, b, c)
oc
```

This can be implemented by forking threads on processors lb through ub.

After the transformations described above have been performed, every concurrent statement can be executed by a simple fork/join. The implementation of fork/join is architecture dependent, but it can be encapsulated in a single run-time support routine, co_stmt, which is invoked by the parent thread to execute a concurrent statement. The arguments to co_stmt are

- a flag to indicate whether concurrent statment is to be executed using multiprogramming or true parallelism,

- the address of the scheduler procedure, and

- the arguments to the scheduler, except for the processor number:

    - a reference to the procedure that encapsulates the body of the concurrent statement,

    - the quantifiers of the concurrent statment, and

    - the optional parameters of the scheduler, if there are any.

The co_stmt routine allocates space for environments, copies the arguments into the appropriate places and fills in the appropriate processor number in each environment. Then it creates threads to execute the scheduler, one per environment, and starts the threads. When all the threads terminate, the concurrent statement is finished and co_stmt returns.

A typical implementation of co_stmt is as follows. Each processor executes a server that services requests to start concurrent statements. The co_stmt routine broadcasts a request to this server, passing the necessary parameters, and then waits for the threads to terminate.

Barriers are implemented by invoking the run-time support routine **barrier**. The implementation of barriers is also architecture dependent; methods of implementing barriers on various architectures are discussed in, for example, [27, 55, 56].

5.2.3   Implementing Delegation

Delegation is implemented by simple macro expansion. A generic procedure such as

> **proc** T
>   ... **delegate** t...
> **end**

is translated into one procedure for each operation in T. The **delegate** statement translates to an invocation. For example, the procedure above is translated into a series of procedures, one for each operation exported by the resource T. If T exports operations t_1 through t_n, the translation of the procedure above will yield n procedures, each of the form

> **proc** t_k(arg, ...)
>   ...t.t_k(arg, ...)...
> **end**

The formal parameter lists are taken from the operation declarations of resource T.

Generic input statements are handled similarly. For example,

> **in** T → **delegate** t **ni**

is translated to an input statement with one arm for each operation exported by resource T:

> **in** t_1(arg, ...) → t.t_1(arg, ...)
> []   t_2(arg, ...) → t.t_2(arg, ...)
> ...
> []   t_n(arg, ...) → t.t_n(arg, ...)
> **ni**

Again, the formal parameters lists are taken from the operation declarations of T.

5.2.4 Translating Input Statements

Input statements are translated into invocations of run-time support routines. Par's input statements are essentially identical to those in SR; thus the description here is quoted almost verbatim from the description in [11].

Classes are fundamental to the implementation of input statements. They are used to identify and control conflicts between threads that are trying to service the same invocations. Classes have a static aspect and a dynamic aspect. A static class of operations is an equivalence class of the transitive closure of the relation "serviced by the same input statement." At compile time, the compiler groups operations into static classes based on their appearance in input statements. At run-time, actual membership in the (dynamic) classes depends on which operations in the static class are extant. For example, an operation declared local to a process joins its dynamic class when the process is created and leaves its dynamic class when the process completes execution. The run-time support represents each dynamic class by a class structure, which contains a list of pending invocations of operations in the class, a flag indicating whether or not some process has access to the class, and a list of threads that are waiting to access the class. Each operation table entry points to its operation's class structure.

At most one process at a time is allowed to access the list of pending invocations of operations in a given class structure. That is, for a given class, at most one process at a time can be selecting an invocation to service or appending a new invocation. Processes are given access to both pending and new invocations in a class structure in first-come/first-served order. Thus, a process waiting to access the invocations will eventually obtain access as long as all functions in synchronization and scheduling expressions in input statements eventually terminate.

The run-time support provides seven routines that the generated code uses for input statements. These routines are tailored to support common cases of input statements and have straightforward and efficient implementations. They are:

access(*class*). Acquire exclusive access to class, which is established as the current class structure for the executing process. That process is blocked if another process already has access to class. The run-time support will release access when this process blocks in trying to get an invocation or when this process executes remove (see below).

get_invocation(). Return a pointer to the invocation block the executing process should examine next. This invocation is on the invocation list in the current class structure of the executing process; successive calls of this routine return successive invocations. If there is no such invocation, the run-time support releases access to the executing process's current class structure and blocks that process.

get_named_inv(op_ref). Get the next invocation of operation op_ref in the executing
   process's current class; a pointer to the invocation block is returned.

get_named_inv_nb(op_ref). Get an invocation of op_ref. This routine is identical to
   get_named_inv except that it does not block the executing process if no invocation is found; instead it returns a null pointer in that case. It is used when the
   input statement contains a scheduling expression.

remove(invocation). Remove the invocation block pointed at by invocation from the
   invocation list of the executing process's current class. The run-time support
   also releases access to the executing process's current class structure.

input_done(invocation). Inform the run-time support that the generated code has finished executing the command body in an input statement and is therefore finished with the invocation block pointed at by invocation. If that invocation was
   called, the run-time support passes the invocation block back to the invoking
   process and awakens that process.

recv(class). Get and then remove the next invocation in class. This routine is equivalent to the sequence

```
access(class)
invocation := get_invocation()
remove(invocation)
```

   Hence, it returns a pointer to an invocation block. It is used for simple input
   statements and for **receive** statements.

The ways in which these routines are used by the generated code is illustrated below by
four examples. More complicated input statements are implemented using appropriate
combinations of the routines.

   Consider the simple input statement:

   in q(x) →   ... **ni**

This statement delays the executing process until there is some invocation of q, then
services the oldest such invocation. (Note that **receive** statements expand into this
form of input statement.) For this statement, if q is in a class by itself, the generated
code executes

   invocation := recv(q_class).

If q is not in a class by itself, the generated code executes

```
access(q_class),
invocation := get_named_inv(q),
remove(invocation).
```

In either case, the generated code then executes the command body associated with q, with parameter x bound to the value for x in the invocation block, and finally executes

```
input_done(invocation).
```

Second, consider:

in q(x) → ... [] r(y, z) → ... **ni**

This statement services the first pending invocation of either q or r. Note that q and r are in the same class because they appear in the same input statement. Here, the generated code first uses

```
access(q_class)
```

and then

```
invocation := get_invocation()
```

to look at each pending invocation in the class to determine if it is an invocation of q or r (there might be other operations in the class). If the generated code finds an invocation of q or r, it calls

```
remove(invocation),
```

then executes the corresponding command body with the parameter values from the selected invocation block, and finally executes

```
input_done(invocation).
```

If the generated code finds no pending invocation of q or r, the executing process blocks in get_invocation until an invocation in the class arrives. When such an invocation arrives, the run-time support awakens the process, which then repeats the above steps.

As the third example, consider an input statement with a synchronization expression:

in q(x) **and** x > 3 → ... **ni**

This statement services the first pending invocation of q for which parameter x is greater than three. The generated code first uses

> access(q_class)

to obtain exclusive access to q's class. The generated code then uses

> invocation := get_invocation()

or

> invocation := get_named_inv(q)

to obtain invocations of q one at a time; the first routine is used if q is in a class by itself, otherwise the second is used. For each such invocation, the generated code evaluates the synchronization expression using the value of the parameter in the invocation block. If the synchronization expression is true, the generated code notifies the run-time support of its success by calling

> remove(invocation),

executes the command body associated with q, and calls

> input_done(invocation).

If the synchronization expression is false, the generated code repeats the above steps to obtain the next invocation.

Finally, consider an input statement with a scheduling expression:

> **in** q(x) **by** x → ... **ni**

This statement services the (oldest) pending invocation of q that has the smallest value of parameter x. In this case, the generated code uses the same steps as in the previous example to obtain the first invocation of q. It then evaluates the scheduling expression using the value of the parameter in the invocation block; this value and a pointer, psave, to the invocation block are saved. The generated code then obtains the remaining invocations by repeatedly calling

> invocation := get_named_inv_nb(q).

For each of these invocations, the generated code evaluates the scheduling expression and compares it with the saved value, updating the saved value and pointer if the new value is smaller. When there are no more invocations (i.e., when get_named_inv_nb returns a null pointer), psave points to the invocation with the smallest scheduling expression. The generated code acquires that invocation by calling remove(psave),

then executes the command body associated with q, and finally calls

input_done(psave).

Note that synchronization and scheduling expressions are evaluated by the generated code, not the run-time support. This is done for two reasons. First, these expressions can reference objects such as local variables for which the run-time support would need to establish addressing if it were to execute the code that evaluates the expression. Second, these expressions can contain invocations; it would greatly complicate the run-time support to handle such invocations in a way that does not cause the run-time support to block itself. A consequence of this approach to evaluating synchronization and scheduling expressions is that the overhead of evaluating such expressions is paid for only by threads that use them.

5.2.5 Replacing Operators with Invocations

Every Par operator except ← is equivalent to an invocation. This equivalence is defined by **overload** declarations. Some overload declarations are built-in; others are user specified. Overload declarations are, in effect, rules for tree rewriting. A typical overload declaration is as follows:

overload a + b ⇒ sum(a, b)

The effect is that any subtree of the form a + b, where a and b are arbitrary subtrees, is replaced by an invocation node that invokes sum with the arguments a and b.

A single, bottom-up pass over the tree suffices to replace all expressions by their corresponding invocations. Each interior node is compared with all overload patterns. If the node's operator name matches the operator on the left-hand side of an overload pattern, the subtree rooted at the node is replaced. The children of the node become part of the new subtree. Figure 5.5 contains a portion of the syntax tree in Figure 5.6, with the expression foo := 3 + 4 rewritten as an invocation.

The naming statement (←) is implemented by copying references. The only complication arises when a naming statement involves a subtype relationship between resource objects. For example, suppose that resource A has the specification

resource A
    op x()
end

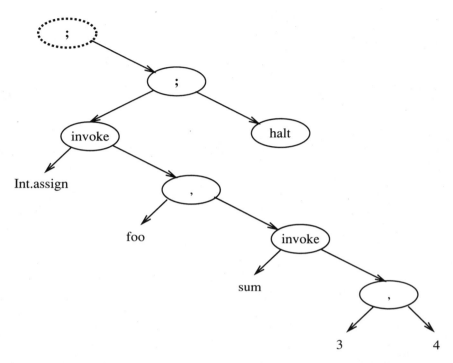

Figure 5.5: A portion of the syntax tree with expressions replaced by invocations.

and that B has the specification

```
resource B
    op x()
    op y()
end
```

Resource B is a subtype of resource A, so the naming statement

a ← b

is legal. It is implemented by projecting the operations of B onto the operations of A. A reference to an instance of A will consist of two pointers (e_A, x_A) and a reference to B will consist of three pointers (e_B, x_B, y_B). Although both resources export an operation named x, the code for these operations is different; thus the address of the code is also different. The naming statement discards the operations in B that do not appear in A. The effect is that after the naming statement, a will be consist of the pair (e_B, x_B).

5.2.6 Assigning Types

The type phase assigns types to those nodes in the tree that represent values. It also reports type errors. This is done in two stages. First, a pre-order traversal of the parse tree adorns identifier and constant nodes with their types. The type of a constant is implicit in its textual representation. The type of an identifier is determined by the most recent (innermost) declaration of that identifier. If a declaration has an implementation clause, the concrete type is used instead of the abstract type. During this pass, undeclared identifiers are detected and reported.

A second pass in the type phase assigns types to invocation nodes of the abstract syntax tree. During this phase, overloaded operations are resolved. This is done in a bottom-up fashion; the type of an invocation node depends on the name of the operation and the types of its arguments. (This is in contrast to languages such as Ada [9], where overloading resolution is much more difficult since the type of an invocation can depend not only on the types of the actual parameters but on the way in which the invocation is used.) To emphasize the fact that operation names are translated to specific procedures in the generated code, we use the notation

> Res!opname

to refer to the procedure that implements operation **opname** exported from resource **Res**.

The result of the type phase is that all nodes in the abstract syntax tree that represent values are adorned with their proper types. If type errors are found, the compilation process stops after this phase. Figure 5.6 contains the syntax tree of Figure 5.5 adorned with types. The types are shown in boxes next to the values to which they refer.

5.2.7 Expanding Invocations

The invocation phase translates each operation invocation into a simple procedure call, either to code that represents the operation or to a run-time support procedure. This involves building an invocation block and transferring control to the code that implements the invoked operation.

Invocation blocks are not part of the Par language; here they will be denoted by double square brackets:

> [[declaration; ...]]

An invocation block consists of a series of declarations. The first declaration in every invocation block is a parent pointer; that is, a reference to the environment in which the operation will execute. We call this object **pptr**. The rest of the invocation block consists of declarations of formal parameters. If a formal parameter is a reference,

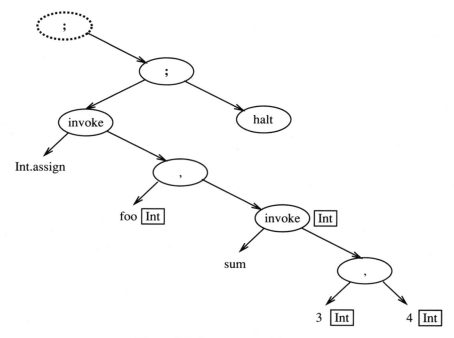

Figure 5.6: Syntax tree with types.

then the actual parameter appears on the right-hand side of a renaming statement. If the formal parameter is a resource or record type, the actual parameter appears as the initial parameter.

For example, suppose that a resource **Res** is declared as follows:

> **resource Res**
>   **op** foo(i : Int, s : **ref**⟨Real⟩, **optional** d : Real(0.0))
> **body**
>   m, n : Int
>   ...
> **end**

If r is an instance of **Res**, and if foo is invoked as

> r.foo(a, b)

then the invocation block corresponding to this invocation is

[[pptr : **ref**⟨Res⟩ ← r
    i : Int(a)
    s : **ref**⟨Real⟩ ← b
    d : Real(0.0)]]

The reference **pptr** will be used in the body of **foo** to access resource variables **m** and **n**. For example, in the function that implements **foo**, **m** will translated into **pptr.m**. The other items in the invocation block are used to access the actual parameters, including the default parameter **d**, which is initialized with its default value since an actual parameter has not been provided.

The way that invocation blocks are allocated and transmitted to the invoked operation depends on the kind of invocation (synchronous or asynchronous) and whether the invocation is local. If the invocation is synchronous and local, the invocation can be implemented as a procedure call. The invocation block is allocated and built on the stack of the invoking thread. The invoked operation then uses the invoker's stack, thus avoiding the overhead of allocating a new stack and copying the invocation block onto it.

If the invocation is asynchronous and on the same processor, the invocation will result in a new thread that executes the operation. The invoker allocates the stack for the new thread and builds the invocation block on that stack. Then the invoker calls a run-time support procedure **create_thread**, passing the address of the new stack and the address of the procedure. The procedure **create_thread** creates a new thread with the specified stack and puts a thread descriptor on the ready list for execution.

If the invocation is not local, the invocation block is built in a block of memory obtained from the run-time support. The memory block is obtained by invoking the run-time support routine **alloc_inv_block**. This allows the run-time support to allocate, in addition to the invocation block, space for any header information that may be necessary. After the invocation block has been built in the allocated block, run-time support routine **remote_inv** is called with the address of the block. This routine copies the invocation block to the local memory of the remote processor and performs the invocation. (If the computer is a UMA machine, copying the invocation block to the local memory of the remote processor will be a null operation since all memory is local to all processors.)

5.2.8 Elaborating Declarations

Par objects are either *primitive* or *nonprimitive*. Primitive types include representations, references, operations, the built-in resources **Vector** and **IdVector**, and records that contain only primitive types. All other objects are nonprimitive. The elaboration phase reduces each declaration of a nonprimitive object to series of primitive declarations and invocations.

A resource declaration is elaborated by substituting for the resource a record containing the (elaborated) declarations that appear at the top level of the resource. This is followed by an invocation of the initial procedure of the resource, if one exists.

Here is an example. Suppose that a stack resource appears as follows:

```
resource Stack⟨T⟩
    op push(T)
    op pop() returns T
    op initial(Int)
body
    stk : ref⟨Vector⟨T⟩⟩
    ptr : Int
    proc initial(size : Int)
        stk ← Vector⟨T⟩(1, N)
        ptr := 0
    end
    proc push... end
    proc pop... end
end
```

Further suppose the following declaration of a stack instance:

```
s : Stack⟨Int⟩(10)
```

This declaration will be translated into the following record declaration and invocation:

```
s : Env_Stack_of_Int
s.initial(10)
```

Here the type Env_Stack_of_Int is a record that contains the top-level declarations in Stack:

```
record Env_Stack_of_Int
    stk : ref⟨Vector⟨T⟩⟩
    ptr : Int
end
```

References are primitive types, so the first declaration in Env_Stack_of_Int is not elaborated further. However, Int is a resource, so the second element of the record is itself transformed to a record containing the declarations contained at the top level of the standard Int resource. This results in the declaration

```
record Env_Stack_of_Int
    stk : ref⟨Vector⟨T⟩⟩
    ptr : Env_Int
end
```

The definition of the record Env_Int depends on the implementation of Int; we will assume that it is primitive.

Also, an invocation of the initial operation of Int is inserted. The result is the following code sequence:

```
s : Env_Stack_of_Int
s.ptr.initial()
s.initial(10)
```

Notice that the objects declared inside Stack are initialized before Stack itself.

The result of the elaboration phase is that each declaration of a resource instance is changed to a declaration of a record that represents the internal representation of the resource. This declaration is followed by an invocation of an initial operation.

Elaborating a declaration can result in the production of additional invocations, each of which may, in turn, produce its own invocation block. This recursive expansion process terminates since every object ultimately is implemented in terms of primitive objects. Each step in the recursive expansion removes one layer of abstraction from the underlying representations.

5.2.9 Generating Code

The transformations described in the previous sections convert Par programs to a simple canonical form. The code consists of a number of sequential procedures. The main procedure has the same name as the program and is invoked on the main processor when the program starts. The sequential program includes declarations of primitive objects, procedure calls, and invocations of run-time support routines to accomplish thread creation, synchronization, and communication. Thus, code generation is reduced to the problem of generating code for sequential programs, which is a well-understood process.

A possible strategy for a portable Par compiler is to generate, for each sequential procedure, a function in some sequential language such as C [69]. Then the compiler for the sequential language performs code generation.

```
program example
   n : 1000
   v : Vector⟨Real⟩(1, n) {use BlockVector}
   s : Int(0.0) {use AccRealSum}
   co i := 1 to n {scheduler block} →
       s + := v[i]
   oc
end
```

Figure 5.7: An example program

5.3 An Example

In this section we demonstrate how the various phases of the program work by compiling a simple example by hand. The first two phases of the compiler are straightforward so for readability we will omit them and work with the program text instead of a parse tree.

Figure 5.7 contains the original program. It is a simple program that sums the elements of a vector. The identifier n is the constant 1000. The identifier v is a real-valued vector, implemented as a BlockVector (Section 3.6.3). The object s is an accumulator (Section 3.2.4). The concurrent statement is scheduled using the scheduler block (Section 3.2.2).

5.3.1 Simplifying the Concurrent Statement

The first transformation rewrites the concurrent statement so to use the scheduler id_scheduler. This transformation, described in Section 5.3.1, results in the following concurrent statement:

```
co p := min_proc() to max_proc() {scheduler id_scheduler} →
   block(cobody, p, 1, n)
oc
```

(Here cobody is a new identifier, unused elsewhere in the program.) Also, the procedure cobody is defined to be the body of the concurrent statement:

```
proc cobody(i : Int)
   s + := v[i]
end
```

```
program example
  n : 1000
  v : Vector⟨Real⟩(1, n) {use BlockVector}
  s : Int(0.0) {use AccRealSum}
  proc cobody(i : Int)
    s + := v[i]
  end
  co_stmt(true, block, cobody, 1, n, 1)
end
```

Figure 5.8: Program example after translation of concurrent statements.

In the body of the scheduler block, the statement

chore(expr)

will be translated into an invocation of cobody.

In this form, the concurrent statement can be implemented by invoking the run-time support routine co_stmt. In this case, the parameters to co_stmt are as follows:

- a flag that indicates that the concurrent statement is to be executed using true parallelism,

- the address of the scheduler block,

- the arguments to the scheduler, except the processor number:

  - a reference to cobody, and

  - the quantifier of the concurrent statement, in this case (1,n,1).

Thus the concurrent statement is replaced by the definition of cobody followed by an invocation of co_stmt. Figure 5.8 contains the resulting program.

5.3.2 Rewriting Expressions

In this phase, expressions involving operators are rewritten into equivalent invocations. The only operator expression in this example is

$s + := v[i]$

The first step is to use the built-in overload declaration

vec[i] $\Rightarrow$ vec.index(i)

to rewrite the index expression. After this transformation the expression becomes

s + := v.index(i)

Now the overload expression

a + := b $\Rightarrow$ a.sum_assign(b)

comes into play and the expression is rewritten as follows:

s.sum_assign(v.index(i))

5.3.3   Assigning Types

In this phase types are assigned to each value in the parse tree and also resolves over-loaded operations. This has the effect of replacing operation invocations with appro-priate procedure calls. The first argument of such a procedure call is the parent pointer for that invocation. For example, the expression

s.sum_assign(v.index(i))

is translated to

AccRealsum!sum_assign(s, BlockVector!index(v, i))

Here, AccRealSum!sum_assign, is the procedure that implements the sum_assign operation of resource AccRealSum. These are implemented as traditional procedure calls. (Built-in resources export predefined functions, which are not translated to pro-cedure calls, but instead substituted in-line.)

5.3.4   Expanding Invocations

The next step is to translate operation invocations into simple procedure calls. The first invocation is to the initial operation of BlockVector:

BlockVector!initial(v, 1, n)

The first item in an invocation block is a reference to the object in which the invoked operation resides. In the case of an operation declared in a resource, this is a reference to the resource instance. In this case the first item in the invocation block is a reference to the representation of v. The other two items are the parameters 1 and n. Thus the invocation block is as follows: declarations:

```
program example
  n : 1000
  v : Vector⟨Real⟩ {use BlockVector}
  call BlockVector!initial
  [[pptr : ref⟨BlockVector_of_Real⟩ ← v
    lb : Int(1)
    ub : Int(n)]]
  s : Real {use AccRealSum}
  call AccRealSum!initial
  [[pptr : ref⟨AccRealSum⟩ ← s
          r : Int(0) ]]
  call co_stmt
  [[parallel : Bool(true)
          sched_name : ref⟨op(...)⟩ ← block
          cb : ref⟨op(...)⟩ ← cobody
          lb : Int(1)
          ub : Int(n)
          step : Int(1) ]]
end
```

Figure 5.9: Program example with operation invocations simplified

---

```
[[pptr_ref : ref⟨Stack⟨Int⟩⟩ ← v
  lb : Int(1)
  ub : Int(n) ]]
```

The actual parameters—the constants 1 and n—are used as initial parameters to the declarations of the formal parameters lb and ub. Thus the invocation is translated to

```
call BlockVector!initial
    [[pptr : ref⟨BlockVector_of_Real⟩ ← v
  lb : Int(1)
  ub : Int(n) ]]
```

The other invocations are translated similarly; the resulting program is shown in Figure 5.9.

5.3.5   Elaborating Declarations

Now declarations are elaborated to yield primitive declarations. The first declaration is a constant declaration of type Int_rep. (Integer literals have type Int_rep.) Thus the declaration is already in primitive form.

The declaration of v is first translated to

$$\text{v} : \text{BlockVector} \langle \text{Real} \rangle (1, \text{n})$$

by substituting the concrete resource for the abstract resource. Then, using the implementation of BlockVector in Section 3.6.3, we translate the declaration to

$$\text{v} : \text{Env\_BlockVector\_of\_Real}$$
$$\text{BlockVector\_of\_Real!initial}(1, \text{n})$$

where the record Env_BlockVector_of_Real contains the top-level declarations of the resource BlockVector:

> **record** Env_BlockVector_of_Real
>   block : IdVector⟨**ref**⟨Matrix⟨T⟩⟩⟩
>   glb, gub, lb, ub : Private⟨Int⟩
> **end**

The first field is primitive, but the others are further elaborated, using the definition of Private (Section 2.9). The result is as follows:

> **record** Env_BlockVector_of_Real
>   block : IdVector⟨**ref**⟨Matrix⟨T⟩⟩⟩
>   glb, gub, lb, ub : Env_Private_of_Int
> **end**

where Env_Private_of_Int is the record

> **record** Private_of_Int
>   rep : IdVector⟨Int⟩
> **end**

```
program example
  n : 1000
  v : Env_BlockVector_of_Real
  call BlockVector!initial
[[pptr : ref⟨BlockVector_of_Real⟩ ← v
  lb : Env_Int(1)
  ub : Env_Int(n) ]]
  s : Env_AccRealSum
  call AccRealSum!initial
[[pptr : ref⟨AccRealSum⟩ ← s
        r : Env_Int(0) ]]
  call co_stmt
[[parallel : Env_Bool(true)
        sched_name : ref⟨op(...)⟩ ← block
        cb : ref⟨op(...)⟩ ← cobody
        lb : Env_Int(1)
        ub : Env_Int(n)
        step : Env_Int(1) ]]
end
```

Figure 5.10: Program example after elaboration of declarations

The resource IdVector is primitive, so the expansion ends.

The other declarations, including those in the invocation blocks, are expanded similarly; for the sake of brevity, we omit the details. The final result of all this expansion is shown in Figure 5.10. Notice that the integers in the invocation blocks have been reduced to representations. Since initialization of representations is built in, the expansion process stops there.

The calculation specified by the program contained in Figure 5.10 can be described as follows.

1. First, the initial thread allocates an initial environment that will contain n, v, and s.

2. The constant Int_rep 1000 is copied into the initial environment.

3. An invocation block for the procedure that implements the initial operation of BlockVector is allocated. Since this is a synchronous invocation on the same processor, the invocation block will be allocated and built on the stack of the main thread.

4. The procedure that implements the initial operation of BlockVector is invoked. The execution of the body of this procedure is not discussed here.

5. Steps 3 and 4 are repeated for the initial operation of AccRealSum. Again, we do not describe the execution of the body of the initial procedure.

6. Steps 3 and 4 are repeated again for the run-time support routine co_stmt:

   - The co_stmt routine allocates one environment on each processor and copies into each environment the processor number, a pointer to cobody, and the quantifiers. Also, as an optimization, it copies into each environment the immutable objects in the parent environment, including n and the offset of several IdVectors.

   - The co_stmt creates a thread for each environment and makes them runnable. The threads each execute the scheduler block.

   - During the execution of block, the threads execute **chore** statements by invoking the procedure referred to by cobody. This procedure accesses the local element of several IdVectors.

   - When all the threads have terminated, the co_stmt routine terminates.

7. Since the call to co_stmt is the last statement in the program, the program terminates.

Notice that, due to replication of immutable objects in sub-environments, the only non-local activity in this calculation is the fork/join executed by co_stmt.

5.4   Summary

We have described how Par programs can be translated into sequential code. To execute a program, this sequential code is loaded on each processor of the computer. Then the run-time support is initialized. On multicomputers, a mem_server is started on each processor to provide data access to other processors. Finally, execution of the program begins by executing a single thread on one processor. The computation spreads to the other processors when the main processor executes run-time support routines that create new threads.

The programmer controls where data is stored and how it is accessed; the model of computation does not hide the location of data from the programmer. In particular, the programmer can control, by means of annotations, where and when remote data access is required.

Par's low-level tasking, interprocess communication, and synchronization mechanisms are nearly identical to those in SR [10, 11]. As in SR, operations are invoked

Effect	Invocation+ Service	Vax			Sun	
		8600	785	780	3	2
Procedure call	call+proc	0.0084	0.038	0.046	0.0086	0.024
Rendezvous	call+in	0.342	1.03	1.54	0.89	2.27
Dynamic process creation	send+proc	0.477	1.33	1.95	1.15	2.96
Asynchronous message passing	send+in	0.200	0.573	0.814	0.680	1.73
Semaphore	P+V	0.024	0.076	0.100	0.03	0.08

Figure 5.11: Time (in milliseconds) required to generate and service invocations using SR's run-time support. Adapted from [13], Table II, page 887.

by call or send and are serviced by procedure or input statements. The SR run-time support mechanisms have been implemented on many computer architectures, including both shared- and distributed-memory computers. Atkins and Olsson [13] studied the performance of the SR run-time support. Figure 5.11, adapted from [13, Table II, page 887], summarizes some of their results. The times in Figure 5.11 include the cost of initializing the run-time support, creating instances of the programs resources, and executing loop control. (Each program generates and services 100,000 invocations.) The times to not include the cost of context switching, except for rendezvous, where two context switches are necessary.

For comparison, a parameterless procedure call in C requires about 0.005 ms on a Vax 8600. Thus we expect a Par procedure call to require about 1.6 times as long as a C procedure call. The overhead is due to the implicit parent pointer that is passed with every procedure call.

Chapter 6

Related Work

As was pointed out in Chapter 1, any language for parallel computation on MIMD computers must accomplish several objectives:

- parallelism must be found,

- the available parallelism must be tailored to fit the target computer,

- tasks must be assigned to processors, either statically or dynamically, and

- since tasks usually are not entirely independent, management of shared data must be arranged.

This chapter describes a variety of approaches to parallel programming on MIMD computers and compares them to the Par approach. First, we discuss parallelizing compilers for sequential programming languages. Such compilers attempt to automate all the steps mentioned above; thus we use the discussion of parallelizing compilers as a basis for pointing out the difficulties inherent in automating each of these steps.

Second, we discuss the use of declarative programming languages for parallel programming. We point out that, although these languages avoid some of the difficulties encountered in parallelizing compilers, many of the same problems arise in slightly different guises.

Third, we discuss several explicitly parallel approaches to programming. These approaches give the programmer more control over the calculation than do parallelizing compilers or declarative languages, but they also place a greater burden on the programmer since more details must be specified.

Finally, we discuss several languages that, like Par, use annotations to tailor programs to computers.

6.1 Parallelizing Compilers

One way to write architecture-independent programs is to write sequential programs and let the compiler deal with the architecture. Besides avoiding the need for designing and learning new languages, this approach offers the possibility of executing existing programs on parallel computers. Thus much research has gone into producing parallelizing compilers for traditional languages, notably FORTRAN.

Certainly there is a place for parallelizing compilers. There exists a large amount of working, debugged software that can be made to run faster on parallel machines with the aid of such systems. However, we feel that in the long run the "right" way to code parallel algorithms is in a parallel language. We have several reasons for this belief, some aesthetic, some practical.

First, parallelizing compilers are of little use to designers of parallel algorithms. No parallelizing compiler can infer parallelism that does not exist; it is not sufficient to write a sequential program and hope that the compiler can find a good parallel algorithm hidden inside. Instead, the programmer must conceive of a parallel algorithm, "sequentialize" the algorithm by imposing some arbitrary order on the steps of the algorithm to form a sequential program, and then ask that a compiler "un-sequentialize" the program—i.e., derive the original parallel algorithm from the sequential program. Writing programs in a parallel language avoids the latter two steps. This results not only in simpler compilers, but also in programs that are clearer since they more directly express the underlying algorithm and the intent of the programmer.

Another problem is that current parallelizing compilers are often ineffective at producing efficient parallel programs.[1] We discuss the reasons for this in some detail since many of the problems encountered by parallelizing compilers also arise in other approaches.

6.1.1 Exposing Parallelism

Exposing parallelism, or "parallelizing", is the process of producing an explicitly parallel program from a sequential program. Most research in this area has been done with FORTRAN as the target language. For example, Callahan [31] presents an algorithm for translating sequential FORTRAN programs into fork-join (**co** ... **oc**) parallel programs. The PTRAN system [6, 42] has similar goals. The use of FORTRAN in these projects is due to the importance of FORTRAN to the scientific and engineering computation community; however, most of the research is also applicable to other imperative, sequential languages.

The backbone of parallelizing compilers is *dependence analysis*. This is used to determine constraints on the order of execution of statements in a program. If there are no constraints between two statements, they can be executed in parallel. One form of dependency is *data dependency*. Data dependencies arise when two statements access the same memory location. For example, consider the following two statements:

---

[1]However, for computers that support limited forms of parallelism such as vector (pipelined) processors, automatic compilation techniques are quite successful. For example, PFC [8], is a source-to-source translator that restructures FORTRAN code for vector computers.

```
a := b;
c := a;
```

The second assignment cannot be executed before, or concurrently with, the first because the first modifies a, which is then used by the second. Thus there is a data dependency between the two statements.

The crux of dependence analysis is detecting aliasing between array references. For example, the two statements

```
a[f(i)] := 7;
a[g(i)] := a[g(i)] + 1
```

can be executed simultaneously if it is known that $f(i) \neq g(i)$. Detecting whether there is a data dependency between two statements that contain array references is, in general, undecidable [22]. Much research has been done to detect aliasing between array references in special cases [76, 19, 20, 116, 68, 7, 29, 18, 78]. While this has proven useful in programs where array indices are restricted to simple expressions, it is not a general solution.

Even when it is theoretically possible to determine precise data-dependence information, actually calculating such information is often intractable. Meyers [89] showed that several data flow problems are theoretically intractable (NP-complete) in the presence of common programming mechanisms such as recursion, procedure nesting, and pass-by-reference aliasing. A common source of parallelism in sequential programs is loops. If the iterations of a loop access disjoint data sets, a loop can be transformed into fork-join style parallel code. However, Kennedy has noted [32] that conventional techniques for interprocedural analysis are "too coarse to allow effective detection of parallelism in loops that contain call sites."

Due to these problems, parallelizing compilers do not derive precise dependence information; instead, they use approximation techniques. The result is that opportunities for parallelism are often missed, which results in poor performance. In such cases the programmer must restructure the program to make it easier to parallelize. This tends to lead to unclear programs. Also, it is difficult to know what to change to improve performance because the programmer is not describing a parallel algorithm, but rather is describing a sequential algorithm from which (hopefully) a parallel one can be derived.

In contrast, we advocate the explicit expression of parallelism. Not only does this simplify the compiler, but it makes programs clearer since they more closely resemble the parallel algorithm on which they are based.

6.1.2   Controlling Granularity

It is often the case that the natural parallelism exhibited by a program is in the form of a very large number of very small chores. The number of chores can be orders of magnitude larger than the number of processors, and the execution time for a chore can be on the order of a few instructions. Such calculations are termed *fine-grained*. The matrix addition example (Section 3.1) is a typical fine-grained program. Most parallel computers cannot efficiently execute fine-grained calculations; the multiprogramming overhead overwhelms the speedup due to parallelism. Thus, for efficiency, it is necessary to prune back the available parallelism to fit the computer by combining chores into larger tasks.

Parallelizing compilers must control granularity automatically. However, since determining the execution time of an arbitrary chore is impossible, automatic chore combination is problematic. Even if chore size could be determined or estimated, it is difficult to know which chores should be combined; the best choice can depend on communication patterns or data layout, for example.

In contrast with parallelizing compilers, Par allows the programmer to control granularity explicitly. Chore combination can take into account communication patterns, data layout, and any other special aspects of the algorithm. For example, in the matrix multiplication example (Section 3.3), we partitioned the chores into blocks to match a grid of processors. Then we mapped the data onto the same processor grid. The result was that each processor executed as single task and all data access was local.

6.1.3   Scheduling Tasks

Even after a parallel program of the correct granularity has been found, the problem remains of deciding on a scheduling policy. Again, there are both theoretical and practical difficulties in doing this automatically.

In a distributed system, tasks can be assigned to separate processors or to the same processor. Assigning tasks to different processors allows the tasks to be executed in parallel. However, other considerations favor putting several tasks on the same processor. Tasks typically need to communicate; assigning two tasks that communicate to different processors incurs an overhead due to communication protocols and transmission delays. In addition, if only a single task is assigned to a processor, the processor may be idle for a significant portion of the computation because a task can be blocked because of communication delays, synchronization with other tasks, or I/O delays.

The *optimal assignment problem* is the problem of assigning tasks to processors so as to minimize the total execution time, which is the sum of execution time of the program and the intertask communication times. In this problem, perfect knowledge of both execution time and communication costs is assumed. The optimal assignment problem is NP-complete for three or more processors [114, 115] except in special cases such as tree-connected networks [24]; thus, in the worst case the problem is intractable. This is not as serious as it sounds, because practical techniques have been found that either approximate a solution in polynomial time [28, 45, 106] or that find an optimal solution usually in polynomial time [105].

However, compilers do not have perfect knowledge about either execution times or communication costs. Furthermore, the optimal strategy is not necessarily a static assignment of tasks to processors; it may involve dynamic task migration. The result is that, in practice, parallelizing compilers use heuristic approaches to scheduling. Typically, all task scheduling is done by general-purpose schedulers that perform fairly well in typical cases and poorly in few cases. For many programs, a carefully chosen, hand-crafted scheduler can do better than the general-purpose one, but parallelizing compilers do not allow such schedulers to be written or used.

In contrast, Par gives the programmer control over the scheduling strategy. This approach allows both general-purpose and specialized schedulers. A possible strategy is to specify, initially, a general-purpose scheduler such as fcfs of section 4.1.1. Then, if profiling the code reveals that a particular concurrent statement is being executed inefficiently, that statement can be annotated to use a more specialized scheduler.

6.1.4 Managing Data

As Karp says in [67]:

> "The importance of data management is also a problem for people writing automatic parallelization compilers. To date, our compiler technology has been directed toward optimizing control flow. Such features as common expression elimination, code movement, and dependence analysis for vectorization have been used for many years. Even today, when hierarchical memories make program performance a function of data organization, no compiler in existence changes the data addresses specified by the programmer to improve performance. If such compilers are to be successful, particularly on message passing and hybrid systems, a new kind of analysis will have to be developed. This analysis will have to match the data structures to the executable code in order to minimize memory traffic."

Some progress has now been made in automatic data management. However, like parallelization and scheduling, data management appears to be a difficult problem to automate; progress has been made only on restricted models of computation. We examine two approaches to automatic data management that illustrate some of the difficulties.

Mace [82] considers the problem of choosing static mappings for data structures in parallel programs. Her model is based on the idea of a *shape,* which is a memory storage pattern for a data structure. For example, partitioning the rows of a matrix among memory elements would be one shape, while partitioning by columns would be another. Thus shapes correspond to Par mappings. In Mace's model, a program is represented by a directed *program graph*. Each node is labeled with an operation, which represents a calculation based on the values of its children. Edges are labeled with shapes, which represent the storage pattern chosen for that datum. The cost of executing a node can depend on the operation and also on the shapes assigned to the incoming edges. The total cost of a shape assignment is the sum of the costs of the nodes. Given this model of parallel programs, the problem is to find an optimal shape assignment—an assignment of shapes to edges that minimizes the total cost. Finding such an assignment corresponds to picking a storage pattern for each datum in the program.

This formulation of the memory-management problem is quite restricted. It assumes a collection of pre-existing, static shapes for data, such as storing matrices by row or column. In reality, there are many ways to store data on parallel machines; it may be useful to design a new shape for a data structure for a particular program. In the image-labeling problem of Section 3.4, for example, we invented the shared_edges mapping to solve a specific data-sharing problem. In Chapter 4, instead of specifying static mappings for data, we designed data structures that adapt themselves to the calculation. Such data structures do not fit into Mace's model.

Mace's model also assumes perfect knowledge of both the program graph and the costs associated with nodes. This is unrealistic except in the case of very regular programs. Yet even in this restricted model, Mace shows that finding an optimal shape assignment is NP-complete except for certain restricted kinds of graphs such as trees [82].

An even more restricted form of the data management problem is examined in [90]. The authors discuss the problem of scheduling *delay points* in multi-stage programs. A multi-stage program is a program that consists of a linear sequence of stages. Each stage can contain parallelism, but the stages are executed one at a time in a fixed sequence; more complicated program graphs such as trees, and DAGs are excluded from consideration. A *delay point* is an optional calculation that can be inserted between stages of a program. A delay point could, for example, remap data so that subsequent stages execute more quickly. (This model does not accommodate self-adapting data structures such as those we developed in Chapter 4, which adapt to usage patterns continuously instead of at discrete intervals.) In this model, the execution time of a stage depends on the position of the most recent delay point.

In [90], the authors show that, assuming perfect knowledge about stage performance as a function of delay points, optimal delay point scheduling can be solved in polynomial time by dynamic programming. In real programs perfect knowledge is rarely available; thus the authors also present a heuristic algorithm for scheduling delay points that seems to produce nearly optimal results in test cases. For this result to be generally useful the technique will have to be extended to more general graphs.

In contrast with automatic data management, Par allows the programmer to specify mappings and remappings. Par also allows dynamic and self-organizing data structures, which mutate in response to usage patterns. In the examples of Chapter 3, data management was for the most part static, with occasional "phase changes" in which data movement occurred. This reflected the regular nature of the algorithms. In Chapter 4, data management was usually dynamic because the irregular algorithms presented there had unpredictable data usage patterns.

6.1.5 Summary

Obtaining an optimal solution to any of the four subproblems discussed above is theoretically intractable. Even obtaining a "good" solution is in many cases very difficult; each of these problems is the subject of current research. Since parallelizing sequential programs involves obtaining solutions to all of these problems, we do not believe that automatic translation of sequential programs to parallel form is currently a practical approach to parallel programming.

Also, we also feel that the first problem—exposing parallelism—is best solved by the programmer. Although automatic detection of parallelism has some uses, we feel that parallel algorithms should be written in a parallel language. Writing a parallel algorithm in a sequential language ensures that the program will not clearly reflect the algorithm.

6.2 Declarative Programming Languages

Imperative languages have an implicit state which is modified by programming commands (hence the term *imperative*). John Backus, in his Turing Award Lecture [14], pointed out that imperative languages suffer from the "von Neumann bottleneck"— the single, narrow "tube" that connects the processor, which executes commands, to the memory, which represents the state. The bandwidth of this channel imposes a fundamental limitation on the rate at which information can be produced and stored. In contrast with imperative languages, *declarative* languages have no implicit state; they are instead based on programming with expressions or terms. To some extent, declarative languages specify *what* is being computed rather than *how* it is computed.

There are many models of declarative programming. Applicative programming is based on the lambda calculus [21] and is the basis for languages such as Miranda [113], ALFL [62, 59, 60] and Haskell [63].   Prolog [74, 58] is based on first order logic. Consul [17] and the distributed constraint (dc) family of languages defined in [102] are based on constraint-based programming. Sisal [84] and VAL [2, 85] are based on the dataflow model of computation. Crystal [101, 37, 39, 38] is based on recursion equations. FP [14] is based on functional programming, which is variable-free programming based on functional forms—higher order functions that combine existing functions to give new ones.[2]

---

[2]The term *functional* has several meanings. This definition is a paraphrase of the one given by John Backus, who coined the term for his language FP [14]. However, many people use *functional* as a synonym

All these languages have the desirable property of *referential transparency*: an expression can always be replaced by its value regardless of the surrounding context. For example, in the expression

```
a*b + c*d
```

the product subexpressions can be replaced by their values without regard for the rest of the program. Referential transparency has the effect of making parallelism easy to expose. In the example above, the two products can be calculated concurrently. Things are more complicated in imperative languages. For example, in the C expression

```
sum(product(a,b), product(c,d))
```

it is not necessarily the case that the two products can be evaluated in parallel. The function `product` could change the values of variables other than the parameters; e.g.,

```
product(int a, int b)
{ c = c+1;   return a*b; }
```

This definition of `product` not only returns the product of its arguments, but also modifies the global variable c. Executing two instances of `product` simultaneously could lead to interference and erroneous results.

As a result of referential transparency, declarative programs typically exhibit a large amount of natural parallelism; unlike imperative programs, parallelism is the rule instead of the exception. However, as we have pointed out, exposing parallelism only the first step in creating an efficient parallel program. The problems of granularity control, scheduling, and data management are also important. Referential transparency does not solve these problems. In fact, maintaining referential transparency makes efficient data management even more difficult than in imperative languages.

Consider, for example, the problem of building a histogram from a list of numbers. Given a list of numbers and a function that maps each element of the list to an integer in a range $1 \dots N$, we want to count the number of elements of the list that map to each i, $1 \leq i \leq N$. In an imperative language such as C this is easy:

```
for (i=1; i<=length(sequence); ++i) {
      slot = f(sequence[i])
      histogram[slot] += 1
}
```

---

for *declarative*; i.e., lacking side effects. Others take it to mean "providing first-class functions;" for example, Scheme and ML are often called functional languages even though they are also imperative languages.

In a language without assignment, however, this strategy is impossible since modifying `histogram` is not allowed. Thus a naive applicative implementation of this algorithm creates a new copy of the vector `histogram` each time it is modified; the result will be a very inefficient program.

One way around this problem is to attempt to derive efficient imperative code from assignment-free programs. The Crystal project [37, 101, 38] takes this approach. However, this requires data-dependency analysis, which—as we pointed out in Section 6.1.1—is difficult to do in general. To date, this approach has proven successful only on very regular problems.

Another approach to the problem of data management is to make declarative languages more expressive by adding novel data structures that allow efficient data management yet preserve referential transparency. Id Nouveau [12] has a type constructor called an I-structure that allows arrays to be created incrementally. Elements of I-structures can be created without copying the entire array. However, I-structures do not permit array elements to be redefined once they have been given values; thus I-structures cannot be used to solve the histogram problem.

In summary, declarative languages exhibit natural parallelism, which makes them more amenable to parallel implementation than imperative, sequential languages. However, exposing parallelism is only one of four difficult problems. Controlling granularity and scheduling tasks are just as difficult with declarative languages as they are with sequential, imperative languages. Data management is even more difficult, since the implementation is constrained by the semantics of referential transparency. A promising hybrid approach, which allows user-specified data management and scheduling for declarative programs, is discussed in Section 6.9.2.

6.3 Distributed Programming Languages

Distributed languages can be used for parallel programming. By a *distributed language* we mean a language with logically distributed address spaces. In such languages, processes interact by by some form of message passing instead of by sharing data. For example, CSP [57] uses synchronous message passing, NIL [109, 92] uses asynchronous message passing, Ada [9] uses rendezvous, Cedar [112] uses remote procedure call, and Argus [81] uses atomic transactions. Some distributed languages, such as SR [11, 10], provide several forms of message passing. The family of distributed languages is very large; the reader is referred to [16] for a survey.

Distributed languages are at the opposite end of the spectrum from parallelizing compilers. Where parallelizing compilers attempt to automatically produce efficient parallel code, distributed languages instead provide features that allow the programmer to explicitly specify parallel computations.

Distributed languages work well for programming inherently distributed applications such as distributed operating systems. The primitives of distributed languages have a direct mapping onto the machine primitives of multicomputers. For example, message passing often translates directly to interprocessor (or interprocess) communication. In some ways, distributed languages are the assembly languages of distributed computers: the language primitives directly model the underlying hardware.

However, distributed languages are not ideal for writing portable parallel programs. To implement a parallel algorithm in a distributed language, the algorithm must be explicitly broken into processes of the proper granularity, the processes must be assigned to processors, and the data must be partitioned among the processes. Breaking an algorithm into processes and assigning them to processors is inherently architecture dependent; it depends strongly on aspects of the architecture such as the number of processors, the communication network topology, and communication speed. This is why Par encapsulates such decisions in scheduler annotations, which can be reimplemented or modified for various architectures.

Partitioning data among processes is often burdensome. Sharing data between processes is natural for many problems, but awkward to express in distributed languages; the shared data must be encapsulated in a server process and accessed by message passing. In contrast, Par allows data to be shared naturally. Mapping annotations allow the physical position of the data (i.e., the processor on which it is stored) to be treated orthogonally from the way the data is used.

Distributed languages can be ported to computers with shared memory. However, this does not necessarily mean that programs written in distributed languages are portable. In a distributed language, the way in which code and data is partitioned into processes are decisions that the programmer must make, but these decisions depend heavily on details of the architecture. In addition, some distributed languages allow programmers to assign processes to particular processors. Programs that use such features are not portable since they rely on a particular collection of processors. Finally, distributed languages make it difficult to take advantage of physical shared memory on computers where it is available. For example, on shared memory computers a natural programming technique is to store large arrays or data in global memory and have processors work on different parts of the array at different times. In a distributed language this is difficult to express since each datum must reside in a process.

Distributed object-based languages are a variant of distributed languages in which each datum is encapsulated in a separate manager process, usually called an object. The objects interact by invoking the exported methods (operations) of other objects. A calculation consists of a dynamic network of active, communicating objects. Parallelism arises because many of the objects can be active simultaneously. This model is a generalization of sequential object-oriented languages such as Smalltalk [53], where each datum is encapsulated in a passive object. Many recent languages are based on this idea; for example, Emerald [64], ConcurrentSmalltalk [117, 118], and Actor-based languages [3].

Distributed object-oriented languages avoid, for the most part, the problem of how to partition an algorithm into processes—each datum is, in essence, a separate process. This makes it easy for a large amount of parallelism to be expressed in the program; since objects are active unless waiting for other objects, parallelism is the default instead of the exception.

However, as we have pointed out, exposing parallelism is only part of the problem. Controlling granularity, scheduling, and data management are important to performance. Several approaches to scheduling are possible in distributed object-oriented languages. Emerald allows object migration under programmer control. This is very flexible but entails a large runtime system and a certain amount of overhead. The other alternative, which most distributed object-oriented languages take, is to place and schedule objects automatically. This approach, of course, encounters the problems outlined in Section 6.1: controlling granularity, scheduling, and data management.

6.4 Simulating Shared Memory

On computers with uniform-access shared memory, data management is much simpler than on NUMA computers and multicomputers. This is because placement of data is not an issue on UMA computers. Thus one step toward achieving architecture-independence would be to provide the illusion of a shared, uniform access memory. This section discusses ways in which a uniform shared-memory abstraction can be provided on NUMA and distributed computers.

6.4.1 Distributed Virtual Memory

One attractive possibility is to have the operating system of a distributed or NUMA computer simulate a uniform-access shared memory. The seminal work on this approach was the IVY project [77], which introduced the idea of distributed virtual memory. Ivy implements a shared virtual address space on a collection of Apollo workstations connected by an Ethernet. Performance measurements showed that the system produced almost linear speedups for programs that displayed a high degree of locality of reference.

The IVY system uses demand paging to simulate shared memory. If a processor attempts to access a page of memory that does not reside on the current processor, a page fault occurs. To service the page fault, the operating system locates the page, moves it to the current processor, and then allows the program to proceed. To provide parallelism while maintaining the semantics of shared memory, IVY allows many processors to have a read-only copy of a page simultaneously, but only one processor to have a copy that can be written. This means that the first time a page is written all other copies of the page must be located and invalidated.

The idea of using demand paging to implement uniform-access shared memory has also been applied to NUMA computers, including the IBM ACE multiprocessor [26] and the BBN Butterfly Plus [47]. Some of the issues involved in implementing uniform-access memory on NUMA computers are discussed in [103].

Using distributed virtual memory as a basis for parallel computation has several problems. First, it relies heavily on locality of reference for its efficiency. Algorithms that do not exhibit good locality of reference will not run efficiently since a large fraction of memory references will result in page faults. Unfortunately, the notion of locality of reference is foreign to the uniform-access memory model. Thus the UMA model of computation ignores certain important aspects of real multicomputers, and can mislead the programmer into writing inefficient programs. This issue is discussed in [108].

In contrast, Par's model of computation makes data locality explicit. Par without annotations can be thought of as providing a UMA model of computation, while the annotations allow locality of objects to be specified by the programmer for efficiency.

Another problem with using paging to simulate uniform-access memory is "false sharing" [26]. False sharing occurs when a single page contains two classes of data that should be put in different memory segments. For example, in a grid computation the best way to schedule the computation is often to partition the grid among the processors and have each processor work on a different piece of the grid. It is unlikely (without special programming tricks) that the grid partitions will fall evenly on page boundaries, nor is there a way to specify this within the UMA model. The result is that some pages will contain portions of the grid that should be mapped to different processors and the page will be repeatedly swapped back and forth between two (or more) processors.

So far this problem has been addressed in ad hoc ways, for example, by adjusting array sizes so that page boundaries and partition boundaries coincide. In [26, page 30] the authors say "We found that false sharing could be reduced, often dramatically, by tuning application code." Of course, this requires that the programmer step outside the UMA model and deal explicitly with the NUMA or distributed nature of the computer. Work is in progress to attempt to detect and correct false sharing [25].

The false-sharing problem arises because the unit of communication, the page, is unrelated to the logical objects of the program. Par does not suffer from false sharing since communication is specified in terms of the logical objects in the program.

6.4.2   Weak Shared Memory

The difficulty of providing coherent shared memory on distributed computers has led to several forms of shared memory that have a "weaker" semantics and thus allow a more efficient implementation. Many applications do not require full consistency in shared data. For example, a time-of-day clock can be considered a variable that is shared between the clock interrupt handler and clients of the clock. It is often the case that clients would rather get an approximate time quickly than a more precise time slowly. More generally, weak shared memory allows tasks to get stale copies of shared variables.

Ada [9] has special rules for shared variables that specify that between synchronization points tasks cannot make any assumptions about the order in which other tasks access the data. This has the effect of allowing the implementation to replicate shared variables and only update copies at synchronization points. The means that shared variables must be treated quite differently from other variables. In particular, it is difficult for two tasks to communicate reliably through a shared variable. The fact that shared variables look the same as other variables but have markedly different semantics makes it easy to write erroneous and implementation-dependent code in Ada.

The languages Blaze [73, 86] and Kali [72], discussed further in section 6.9.3, also treat shared variables specially. These languages allow tasks to be spawned in fork-join style by the use of the forall statement. The semantics of shared variables in a forall statement are copy-in, copy-out. For example,

```
forallp i in 1 .. N-1 do
    A[i] := A[i+1]
end;
```

has the effect of "left-shifting" the array A. The array reference on the right-hand side accesses the original array, while reference on the left-hand side is to a copy. In effect, the entire array is replicated before the forall statement begins execution; all read access is to the old copy of the array. When the forall statement terminates, the old copy of the array is replaced by the new copy. In reality, of course, compiler analysis can often detect cases where replication is unnecessary.

In [40], Cheriton describes a concept called *problem-oriented shared memory*. A problem-oriented shared memory is an abstraction that provides *fetch* and *store* operations that are specialized to the particular application it is supporting. These operations provide relaxed forms of consistency that are good enough for the application and cheap to provide. Examples include relaxing cache coherency or maintaining a "sufficiently accurate" value for the time-of-day.

Various forms of weak or problem-oriented shared memory can be implemented in Par, since they are really a form of caching that does not require strict coherence. However, we feel that it is important to distinguish such problem oriented abstractions from more standard ones. It would be a confusing, for example, to implement a "weak array" in which the index operation might return stale data; it is better to use a name other than index to avoid potential confusion.

6.5   Paralations

The paralation model [99] is a collection of constructs that are added to a sequential language to give a parallel language. The paralation model explicitly addresses object locality—objects can be put "close to" one another in the sense of the communication metric. Although the syntax of Paralation Lisp is used in this section, most of the description applies to any paralation language. (It is assumed that basic Lisp syntax is familiar to the reader.)

A *paralation* is a vector-like collection of *paralation sites*. Each paralation site is a collection of *fields*. Each field has a value at each site in its paralation.

Programmers never manipulate paralations directly; instead they manipulate fields. Every paralation has a special index field, which contains, at each site, the index of that site. The make-paralation primitive creates a paralation of the specified size and returns its index field. For example,

```
(make-paralation 10)
```

creates a paralation with ten sites and returns the index field:

```
#F(0 1 2 3 4 5 6 7 8 9)
```

(Fields are denoted like Lisp lists, but with #F prepended.)

New fields can be created from old ones by means of the elwise primitive. For example, consider the following Paralation Lisp fragment:

```
(setq p1 (make-paralation 10))
(setq p2 (elwise (p1) (+ p1 1)))
```

The first line creates a paralation and assigns the index field to p1. The second line operates on the index field p1 element-wise, creating a new field in the same paralation. The new field is obtained by adding one to each element in the field p1; hence, after the second line p2 will have the value

```
#F(1 2 3 4 5 6 7 8 9 10)
```

To create a third field that is the sum of the p1 and p2, the following would suffice:

```
(setq p3 (elwise (p1 p2) (+ p1 p2)))
```

The fields to be operated upon element-wise are enclosed in parentheses after elwise.

The function specified in an elwise is arbitrary; in particular, it can have side effects. However, the order in which sites are computed is not specified. It is an error for side effects to conflict. Implementations of Paralation Lisp are not required to detect such an error, however.

The other basic structure in the paralation model is the *mapping*. A mapping can be thought of as a bundle of arrows between two paralations. Mappings are created by the match primitive, which takes as parameters two fields:

```
(match dest-field src-field)
```

and produces a mapping with an arrow from the source site to the destination site if dest-field and src-field are equal. (Note that, although the arguments are fields, the arrows connect paralation sites, not fields.) For example, consider the Paralation Lisp fragment

```
(setq f1 (make-paralation 6))
(setq f2 (make-paralation 6))
(setq f3 (elwise (f2) (mod (+ f2 3) 6)))
(setq map (match f1 f3)
```

The effect is shown in Figure 6.1. The first line creates a new paralation with six sites and names it f1. The second line creates a second paralation, also with six sites, and names it f2. The third line creates a new field, f3 in the second paralation by an elwise operation. Finally, the mapping map is created. The mapping is the bundle of arrows connecting the two paralations. The arrows link a paralation site of the second paralation to a paralation site of the first if f3 and f1 have the same value at those sites. (The src and dest fields of a mapping can be members of the same paralation.)

Mappings are used as paths to move data. The move primitive, written <-, "pushes" a field through a mapping, creating a new field in the paralation that is the destination of the mapping. Thus, if the arrows form a one-to-one mapping between source and destination sites, move models parallel point-to-point communication. For example, if the situation is as pictured in Figure 6.1, then

```
(<- f3 :by map)
```

creates a new field in the first paralation which is a copy of the field f3 in the second paralation. The mapping map is used to move the data.

The move primitive is more powerful than this, however. If two arrows leave a source site, the data from the source site is duplicated and sent along each arrow. (This models multicast.) If no arrow enters a destination site, a default value can be provided, which will be assigned to the destination. Finally, if multiple arrows enter a destination site, values are combined pairwise by a user-specified, dyadic function. The order in

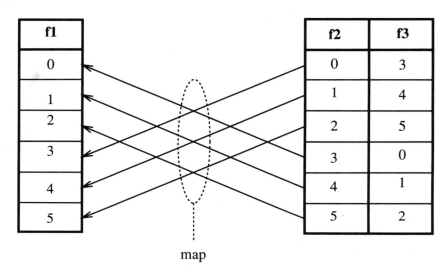

Figure 6.1: A paralation mapping.

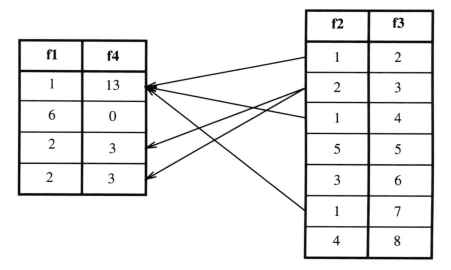

Figure 6.2: A more complicated move

which pairs of arrows are combined on the way to the destination is not specified so combining functions are usually associative. Figure 6.2 contains an illustration of the use of a more general mapping. The mapping was created by the following match:

```
(setq map (match f1 f2))
```

Then `map` was used to create the field `f4` from `f3`:

```
(setq f4 (<- f3
           :by map2
           :with #'+
           :default 0))
```

The + function is specified as the combiner and the default value is specified as zero. Thus element 0 of `f4` is $2 + 4 + 7$, element 1 is 0 since there are no incoming arrows, and elements 2 and 3 are both 3 since the incoming arrows have the same source.

Unlike many other parallel models, the paralation model deals explicitly with locality of communication. It has a three level locality hierarchy: intrasite, intersite, and inter-paralation. Intrasite communication—communication within a paralation site—is the cheapest; communication between sites of a paralation is intermediate in cost; and communication between different paralations is the most expensive. The programmer can also refine the hierarchy somewhat by building *shaped paralations*. A shaped paralation is specified by providing not only a size for a paralation, but a collection of mappings from the paralation to itself. The compiler attempts to lay out the paralation so that these mappings are inexpensive.

Although the concept of locality in paralation languages is explicit, the use of the locality information is left to the compiler. This is both good and bad. It tends to make programs more portable since programs never mention architectural details. On the other hand, it compromises efficiency. On its "native" machine, the Connection Machine, the paralation model of locality has a reasonably straightforward mapping onto the machine (although even there some aspects of the model—such as nested paralations—make memory allocation "quite difficult" [99, page 126]). On other machines the interpretation of the locality information is not at all straightforward. A programmer might, for example, build a grid-shaped paralation to solve the image labeling problem (Section 3.4). The paralation compiler would be responsible for mapping the grid onto the target computer, which might be arranged as a ring or a tree. The best way to map a grid onto a tree is not at all obvious.

The use of virtual architectures in Par allows the same sort of machine independence as paralations. In contrast with the paralation model, however, Par also allows (in fact requires) programmers to specify precisely the way virtual architectures are mapped onto the physical computer. This reflects Par's strategy of providing a flexible framework for building architecture-independent programs instead of providing high-level constructs as primitives.

The paralation model does not address the issue of granularity. The designer of the paralation model assumes [99, page 122] that the target machine has n processors, where n is the size of the largest paralation. This is intended to be accomplished by use of a "virtual processor" facility, by which an arbitrary number of virtual processors are simulated on the available physical processors. On the Connection Machine, this is a reasonable assumption since the Connection Machine is designed to provide virtual processors. On MIMD computers, however, simulating virtual processors can be quite expensive. For example, imagine a paralation program that creates a 100×100, grid-shaped paralation on a computer with only 10 processors. In this situation each processor will have to simulate 1000 virtual processors. This means that each `elwise` applied to the paralation will have a cost of at least 1000 context switches (plus whatever useful work is done). If the `elwise` operation is simple—e.g., add 1 to each element of the paralation—the cost of the context switches will far outweigh the actual work done.

Par, in contrast, allows small chores to be statically combined by the use of schedulers. This allows the 1000 context switches required in the example above to be replaced with a sequential loop from 1 to 1000. Even very light-weight context switches are much more expensive than loop control within a thread.

The paralation model is more general than Par because it addresses both MIMD and SIMD machines. It remains to be seen whether the Par method can be adapted to SIMD computers.

6.6   Futures

Multilisp [94, 95, 96] is an extended version of Scheme [1, 111] that supports explicit parallelism. Multilisp's parallelism is based on the `future` construct. The expression `(future E)`, where E is an arbitrary Multilisp expression, creates a task to execute E and also creates an object that will eventually hold the value of E. This object is called a future. It is initially in an unresolved state since it has not yet been evaluated. When the value of the future is known—when the task associated with the future terminates—the future is resolved and contains the value computed by the task.

The effect of using a future as an operand of some operator has one of two effects, depending on the kind of operator. If the operator is *strict*—that is, if the operator needs the value of its operands—the operator delays until the future becomes resolved. (Of course, if the future has already been resolved there is no delay.) For example, in the expression

```
(+ (future (* a b)) (future (* c d)))
```

the operator + is strict since it requires the arithmetic values of its operands to perform the addition. Thus the expression is delayed until the two futures are resolved. When the futures are resolved the addition takes place.

When used as an operand to a non-strict operator, a future does not cause the operator to delay. For example, in the expression

```
(cons (future (* a b)) 1st)
```

the `cons` operator builds a pair, the first element of which is a pointer to the future value of `(* a b)`. The `cons` operator is not strict since it does not need to know the value of `(* a b)`, merely its location. Thus the `cons` operation is not delayed; it proceeds in parallel with the evaluation of the future. Later, if a strict operator uses this future by accessing the first element of the pair, the operator will be delayed unless the future has meanwhile been resolved.

The future construct is expressive and flexible. Fork-join style parallelism can be simulated by creating a vector of futures and then waiting for all of them to resolve. Other paradigms, such as the producer-consumer model, speculative parallelism (computing values that might be needed later), and "live data structures" [34, pp.345–346] are also easy to express. The use of Scheme, a highly expressive language, as the base language for Multilisp makes it easy to encapsulate the use of futures in higher level constructs.

Multilisp has been implemented on the Concert multiprocessor [95], which is an experimental NUMA multiprocessor with eight processors. The results so far indicate that Multilisp programs run almost n times as fast on n processors as the same program running on one processor. However, this is partly due to the fact that Multilisp runs quite slowly on a single processor; it is not nearly as fast as traditional imperative languages. Also, the creation of a future is a fairly expensive operation; this makes it impractical to use futures to express fine-grained parallelism.

Thus far, Multilisp has not been implemented on distributed memory multiprocessors. Scheduling and data mapping are much more difficult on such computers than on shared-memory computers since the cost of remote references is much higher. Multilisp provides no support for allowing the user to specify scheduling strategies and data mapping. As we have pointed out, these are very difficult problems to solve automatically.

6.7 Generative Communication

The Linda system [4, 35] is a collection of primitives that implement what is called generative communication. The Linda model of parallelism and communication is based on a distinctive memory model called *tuple space*. The conventional memory model, upon which von Neumann languages are based, involves reading and writing words of memory, where the words are accessed by address. In contrast, Linda's memory model is based on adding, reading, and removing tuples of values, which are accessed by content. A process is created when an active (unevaluated) tuple is deposited in tuple space. Unevaluated tuples are similar to Multilisp's futures; they calculate their own value and then become ordinary passive tuples, accessible to other processes.

A Linda tuple is a series of fields. Each field can be either a value or a formal, which is a name and type. Formals are usually used in *templates,* which are described below. Two fields *match* if they both contain identical values or if one contains a value and the other contains a formal of the same type. Two tuples *match* if they have the same number of fields and the fields match pairwise.

Linda's tuple space (TS) is manipulated by four primitives—out, in, rd, and eval—and two variant forms—inp and rdp. Invoking out(t) deposits the tuple t in TS. This operation is asynchronous; the invoking process continues immediately.

Invoking in(s) delays the invoking process until TS contains some tuple t that matches the tuple s (called the template). When a matching tuple is found, any formals in the template s are assigned the values of the matching fields in t. (The tuple t may also have formals, which must match, in type, the corresponding value in the template.) If multiple tuples match s, one is chosen nondeterministically.

Invoking rd has the same effect as invoking in except that the matching tuple is not removed from TS. Invoking eval(t) has the same effect as invoking out(t) except that t is evaluated after, rather than before, it enters TS; executing eval implicitly creates a new process to evaluate the tuple. When evaluation of t is complete it becomes a passive tuple and can be retrieved by in or rd. The variants inp and rdp are like in and rd except that they are non-blocking. If a matching tuple can be found, they return 1 and make formal assignments; if not, they return 0.

Linda has some advantages over Par. Since it is grafted onto (or "injected into") other programming languages, the programmer can program in a familiar language with only a few added primitives. Existing subroutine libraries can be used with Linda programs. In contrast, Par requires the adoption of a new language. (However, see Section 7.2 for a discussion of how the Par method could be adapted to existing languages.) For many algorithms, Linda primitives allow very elegant solutions. For examples of various styles of Linda programs, see [34].

However, Linda also has drawbacks. Linda programs explicitly specify granularity; this tends to make programs architecture dependent. In Linda, the programmer has no control over scheduling and data management. As we have pointed out, these are difficult to do well automatically.

In addition to these problems, which are shared by most other approaches to parallel programming, Linda's tuple space has some problems of its own. The single, global tuple space is a marked violation of the principle of information hiding. Any process can withdraw any tuple from TS, regardless of the intended recipient. A possible solution to this problem is multiple tuple spaces [51]. In contrast, Par provides good information hiding, as do most object oriented languages. (It has also been proposed to add the Linda primitives to object oriented languages [35, 83], but this does not improve the information hiding properties of tuple space, which are independent of the base language.)

For many problems, Linda's notation seems awkward. Consider adding two distributed vectors element-wise. In C-Linda, this might be written as follows:

```
for (i=1; i<= n; i++) {
        rd(a, i, ? a_value);
        rd(b, i, ? b_value);
        eval(V, i, a_value + b_value);
}
```

The Par equivalent,

$$\textbf{co } i := 1 \textbf{ to } n \rightarrow \ v[i] := a[i] + b[i] \textbf{ oc}$$

seems much more natural. Moreover, the C-Linda program above would be quite inefficient since the tasks are very small. A more practical program, in which the vector is stored as blocks to make the program more efficient, would be even less clear. In contrast, the granularity of the Par program can be modified by merely adding a scheduler.

The implementors of Linda are currently working on remedies for the efficiency problems of naive Linda implementations. Some of these ideas are discussed in [50]. It remains to be seen if Linda can be made efficient enough to compete with approaches that offer the programmer low-level control over data placement and communication, especially on fine-grained problems.

6.8   Shared Data Objects

The Orca [15] language is based on the shared data-object model of computing. It is designed for, and has been implemented on, both shared-memory and distributed computers.

Parallelism in Orca is explicit and is specified by the `fork` construct. The statement

```
fork pname(parameters) on pnumber;
```

has the effect of starting a process from a template named `pname` on the processor numbered `pnumber`. Both processes proceed independently. Parameters to processes can be *value* parameters or *shared* parameters. Value parameters are passed by value in the standard fashion. Shared parameters are similar to Par's reference parameters;

the invoked process shares the object with the invoker. The only way an object can be shared between processes is by specifying it as a shared parameter.

An Orca object consists of some private internal data and a collection of externally visible operations. The operations of an object execute indivisibly; thus mutual exclusion is taken care of automatically. An operation consists of a set of boolean guards, each with associated statements. An operation blocks until a guards is true and then executes the associated statements. Since operation guards are required to be side-effect free, operations block only before they begin execution. (This is important since operations must execute atomically.)

Object management is automatic and is performed by the run-time system. Three run-time systems are described in [15]. The first, for shared memory computers, puts shared objects in shared memory and protects each with a lock. Before executing an invocation on a shared object, the invoking process must acquire the object's lock. Then, if a guard is found to be true, the operation proceeds; upon completion the lock is released. If no guard is true, the invoking process is put on a waiting list for that object and the lock is released. Whenever an object is modified, the processes on the waiting list become runnable again and attempt to re-acquire the lock.

The second run-time system runs on distributed computers with a reliable broadcast mechanism; for example, several computers connected to an Ethernet. This system replicates all shared objects on all processors. Read operations lock and use the local copy. Write operations employ a reliable broadcast mechanism to lock and update all copies atomically.

The final version of the run-time system is for the Amoeba operating system. This run-time system uses a more elaborate object-management system. Shared objects are originally placed on the same processor as the process that creates them. When a shared object is passed as a parameter, what is actually sent is a remote reference to the object. The remote processor can execute operations on the object by remote procedure call. If a processor makes frequent read-access to an object, the run-time system may replicate the object on that machine. Thereafter, the object must be modified using a two-phase update protocol. If an object is frequently modified by a processor other than the one on which it resides, the run-time system may move the object to the other processor.

In brief, the Orca approach to parallel programming is to give the programmer control over process placement and interaction while automating data management. Thus Orca allows explicit control over granularity and scheduling, while providing automatic data management.

From the language-design point of view, Orca is a considerably higher-level language than Par. Par is based on the idea that high-level constructs such as atomic operations and data migration should be built using the abstraction mechanisms in the language. Thus Par provides a combination of low-level primitives and facilities for building higher level abstractions. The higher level approach makes Orca simpler to use if it provides what is needed. However, Orca is considerably less flexible than Par. For example, the three strategies for data management mentioned above can all be used to manage Par resources. It is also easy to implement resources that have atomic operations. Par can also be used to implement many data-management policies that Orca does not provide, including objects with non-atomic operations.

Some Orca constructs require interprocedural analysis for efficient implementation. One example is the use of nested objects. Since objects can be nested, a nested operation invocation can cause an operation to block after it has begun execution. This is contrary to the semantics of Orca, which specify atomic execution of operations. The solution, in the general case, is to copy the outer object upon invocation and roll back to the initial object if a nested invocation blocks. This can often, but not always, be avoided by interprocedural analysis. The design of Par attempts to avoid primitive features that require an expensive implementation, either at compile time or execution time.

6.9 Annotating Programs

The section discusses approaches to architecture-independent parallel programming that, like Par, use annotations to achieve efficiency. These approaches differ from each other both in the model provided by the base language and in the power of the annotations.

6.9.1 Data Placement Annotations

An interesting approach to compiling imperative programs is described by Callahan and Kennedy in [33]. (A very similar strategy for annotating Id-Nouveau programs for distributed execution is described in [97].) They describe a method of using data placement annotations to guide the compilation of sequential FORTRAN for distributed computers. Although the paper does not address the problem of shared memory computers, it is clear that the technique could be adapted to those architectures, and would thus provide an architecture-independent language for parallel programming.

The language described in [33] is FORTRAN with extensions to specify data placement. The details of how data placement is done are not important here; the important point is that, for each datum in the program, the programmer assigns an "owner"—a processor on which it will be stored. (If a datum is not assigned an owner, the compiler assigns one.) The owner of a datum is responsible for managing that datum: if the datum is the target of an assignment, the owner performs the modification; if the datum is needed by another processor, the owner sends it.

The semantics of the language are the semantics of standard FORTRAN. In the basic execution scheme, each processor executes every statement. Assignment statements are executed cooperatively. For example, consider the following assignment:

```
a := b + c
```

The owners of b and c send their values to the owner of a. The owner of a waits for the values of b and c, adds them, and modifies a. The processors not involved in this calculation proceed immediately to the next statement. It is proceeding immediately to the next statement that is the basis for parallelism in this approach. For example, when executing a loop, each processor may be able to proceed directly to a different loop iteration.

All the processors must follow exactly the same execution path through the program; thus variables that affect the execution path must be duplicated on all processors. Branching is accomplished by having all the processors calculate the value of the boolean branch condition. Loop variables are duplicated on all processors, so all processors execute the same loops.

The basic compilation mechanism provides correct execution of sequential code on distributed processors, and thus preserves the semantics of FORTRAN. Potential parallelism is exposed at runtime because processors can bypass sections of code in which they do not participate. However, without code reorganization the actual parallelism achieved is rather small. In the unoptimized execution scheme, each processor must check every datum in every statement to determine if it is the owner. Since this check is likely to take as long as actually accessing a local datum, no time is saved. In addition, processors are delayed when they wait for other processors to send data.

The goal of optimization, then, is to minimize the number of ownership checks and synchronization points. The former is primarily a matter of constant propagation. The owner of each datum is fixed, so with enough analysis of the program, it can often be determined a compile time which processor owns which data. Array references, as usual, complicate the picture; aliasing between array references leads to imprecise ownership information. To minimize synchronization, code must be reorganized so that a relatively large amount of work can be done between synchronization points. The authors outline twelve standard optimizations that can be used to this end. (One advantage of this approach to compiling for distributed computers is that most of the well-developed machinery of sequential code analysis is applicable.)

Specifying data placement allows the compiler to avoid issues of data management. Furthermore, the scheduler is specified (albeit indirectly) since the schedule arises from the execution strategy. However, annotating data placement does not solve all the problems with parallelizing compilers. It is still necessary to begin with a program that contains parallelism—the compiler cannot derive parallel code from sequential algorithms. Also, this approach relies heavily on sequential code analysis techniques, which in general can produce only approximate results. Another serious problem is that the data placement, and thus the scheduler, are required to be static. For many problems—such as those described in Chapter 4—static placement and scheduling is not sufficient for good performance.

6.9.2 Annotating Declarative Languages

As was noted in section 6.2, declarative languages in general, and applicative languages in particular, display a large potential for parallelism. However, controlling the parallelism is difficult to achieve automatically. Several proposals have been made to annotate declarative programs to provide control over the parallelism. This strategy has several nice properties. It is very flexible since it does not presume any particular applicative language or architecture. The annotations do not affect the correctness of the program, so changing the annotations is all that is needed for portability. Programs can be debugged on a uniprocessor system that ignores the annotations.

Burton [30] suggests using annotations to control the evaluation order of terms in the lambda calculus; applicative order, normal-order, and mixed-order reductions can be specified using his notation. He also discusses scheduling considerations for evaluating such annotated programs. Burton does not, however, consider explicitly annotating programs to specify on which processor a subexpression should be evaluated.

Hudak [59, 61] advocates *para-functional* programming, which refers to the strategy of annotating subexpressions of pure applicative languages to specify both evaluation order and assignment of subexpressions to processors. He has designed the para-functional language ParAlfl [59, 60], which embodies these ideas. Goldberg describes Alfalfa [54], an implementation of ParAlfl. The target architecture was a 128-node iPSC-386 hypercube. The author found that programs showed good *introspective speedup;* that is, they ran almost n times as fast on n processors as they did on one processor. However, the overall performance was poor compared with imperative implementations of the same algorithms because the programs ran very slowly on a single processor. This reflects the fact we do not yet know how to implement pure applicative languages, especially non-strict languages, efficiently even on uniprocessors.

Annotating declarative programs is a promising area of research. It seems likely that annotations will permit good introspective speedups on both shared-memory and distributed-memory computers. However, a great deal of improvement will have to be made before declarative languages are competitive with imperative languages for general-purpose computing. Data management, especially a solution to the problem of updating large aggregate data structures such as arrays, is particularly important.

6.9.3 Kali

Kali [72] is a set of extensions that can be added to imperative languages to allow compilation on distributed memory computers. The language described here is Kali applied to Blaze [73, 86]. (Work is in progress on a Kali FORTRAN [71].) The result is an explicitly parallel, imperative programming language that supports shared objects on distributed processors. It is similar to Par in that it provides placement and scheduling annotations that allow the programmer to tailor programs to various architectures.

The execution environment for a Kali program is specified by a *processor array*. For example,

```
processors Procs:   array[1..P] with P in 1 ..
max_procs;
```

allocates a one-dimensional array of physical processors numbered 1 ... *P*. The number max_procs is the maximum number of processors that is acceptable; the number *P* is chosen at runtime to be in the range 1 ... max_procs, depending on the number of processors available. Multidimensional arrays can also be declared. It is assumed that the underlying architecture can support multidimensional arrays of physical processors.

Arrays are partitioned by means of a *distribution clause* in their declaration. The distribution clause specifies a distribution pattern for each dimension of the array. A distribution pattern is a function from processors to sets of array elements. The distribution pattern is assumed to partition the array; each element of a distributed array is stored only once. Kali provides notation for several common distribution patterns such as block and block-cyclic; it also provides a mechanism for user-defined distributions. Scalar variables and arrays without distribution clauses are replicated on all the processors.

Parallelism is provided by a forall statement, which is a variant of the "parallel for loop." Scheduling of a forall statement is specified by an on clause; which assigns chores to processors. For example, the forall loop

```
forall i in 1 to N  on A[i].loc do
    A[i] := B[i] + C[i]
end;
```

sets the vector A to the sum of vectors B and C. The value of each A[i] is calculated on the processor that owns A[i], which is denoted A[i].loc.

With regard to data placement, the primary difference between Par and Kali is the generality of the mechanisms provided. Since Kali is designed for numeric computation, it provides placement annotations only for distributed arrays. Par is intended to be a more general purpose language and thus allows arbitrary distributed data structures. Also, Kali assumes that arrays are partitioned; Par allows array elements to be replicated, and provides mechanisms by which programmers can design protocols to handle the replicated data. In Kali, array mappings are static, while in Par arrays (and other objects) can be remapped for efficiency. (However, dynamic array distributions may be added to Kali in the future [71].)

With regard to scheduling, Par and Kali provide almost equivalent power—in either language any chore can be specified to be executed on any processor. However, this information is provided differently in the two languages. Kali schedulers (on clauses) are mappings from chores to processors. Par schedulers are (essentially) mappings from processors to sets of chores. At execution time what is needed is the latter, not the former; each processor must iterate through the chores that are assigned it. This means that, in Kali, a processor must essentially invert the mapping from chores to processors in order to determine which chores to execute. In the case of simple, regular schedulers, which are common in the problem domain for which Kali is designed, the calculation of the inverse chore-assignment function can be done at compile time. In general, however, some execution-time calculation is necessary. As the designers of Kali point out [72], this calculation can sometimes be amortized over more than one execution of the forall statement.

6.9.4 Dino

Dino [98] is a language for writing numerical programs on distributed memory multi-processors. Dino allows distributed data structures to be annotated with *distributions*, which specify how they are to be stored.

Dino programs run on virtual parallel machines termed *environment structures*. An environment structure is an arrangement—an array or a tree, for example—of identical *environments*. Environment structures are created by *environment declarations* in the main program. Each environment can contain local data and procedures as well as *composite procedures*. Composite procedures can be invoked from the main program; this has the effect of simultaneously invoking the composite procedure in each environment of a virtual parallel machine and waiting until all the instances of the composite procedure terminate. Composite procedure call is the only form of parallelism in Dino. This tends to encourage a data-parallel style of programming.

Shared data structures can be distributed over an environment structure. Each element of the data structure can be mapped to one or more environments, depending on how it will be used. For example, an array could be partitioned by rows, columns, or blocks, or it could be distributed as a collection of overlapping blocks to solve problems such as the image-labeling problem in Section 3.4. Distributions can be specified by the programmer or taken from a library of distributions.

Communication between environments is accomplished by reading and writing distributed variables. Dino provides several kinds of access to distributed variables. Local access—read or write—always uses the local copy of the distributed variable, which must be mapped to the environment that is accessing it. Remote access performs communication. Remote write to a distributed variable sends a message containing the new value to each environment to which the variable is mapped. A corresponding remote read on another environment receives the message and assigns it to the local copy.

Both synchronous and asynchronous distributed variables can be specified. With synchronous distributed variables, a remote read uses the oldest unread message and blocks if none is available. With asynchronous distributed variables, remote read uses the most recent unread message if one exists, otherwise the local value is used.

Because of the highly synchronous, data-parallel style of Dino programs, scheduling is not really an issue. Dino's distributions are similar in intent to Par's mappings. However, distributions are written in a special language, not a general programming language. Dino's distributions are more general than those provided in Kali (section 6.9.3) because they are not constrained to be partitions. However, Par's mappings are more general; a Par resource could be designed to emulate an arbitrary Dino distribution; the converse is not true.

6.9.5 Unity

UNITY [36] (which is short for Unbounded Nondeterministic Iterative Transformations) is a computational model and proof system for parallel programming. Although UNITY is not based on annotation, it shares with the other systems in this section the emphasis on incremental development—of beginning with a simple, architecture-independent statement of the algorithm and then developing an efficient program by stepwise refinement.

A UNITY program consists of declarations of variables, specification of their initial values, and a set of guarded multiple assignment statements. Program execution begins in a state satisfying the initial values of the variables and continues forever. In each step, some assignment statement is selected and executed. The selection is nondeterministic and fair. This simple programming model is shown to be powerful and amenable to formal analysis.

In [36] the authors advocate a programming style that, like Par,

> "... separates concerns between *what* on the one hand, and *when, where,* and *how* on the other."

The authors present many examples of how UNITY programs can be mapped onto different architectures. The process of mapping begins with a UNITY program that is correct. By a series of program transformations, the program is transformed into a program suited to a particular architecture. These transformations have a formal basis but they are not automatic.

UNITY is similar to Par in its goal. However, UNITY takes a much different approach to the problem. UNITY adopts an elegant but quite unfamiliar notation, while Par adopts a conventional notation. Mapping a UNITY program to an architecture is done by a series of program transformations, each one of which preserves correctness and moves closer to the final architecture. Tailoring a Par program to an architecture is done by adding annotations that preserve correctness but change the implementation of the high level programming constructs.

The method used in mapping UNITY programs to architectures is more general than tailoring Par programs by annotating them. For example, UNITY programs can be tailored to architectures such as systolic arrays, while Par addresses only MIMD computers. However, Par annotations are easy to apply, while mapping a UNITY program to an architecture requires significant intellectual and creative effort. In a sense, a Par annotation is a specific program transformation of the kind done in UNITY. However, Par supports only certain transformations, such as specifying the implementation of abstract data types or schedulers.

Chapter 7

Conclusions

7.1 Summary

In this book we have addressed the problem of how to write parallel programs that are simultaneously portable, efficient, and clearly written. We have pointed out that each of these aspects is important. Portability is important because rewriting programs for different architectures is expensive and prone to error. Efficiency is important because the main reason for using parallel computers is speed; inefficient programs squander the expensive resources provided by parallel computers. Clarity is important in all programming; unclear programs are hard to write, hard to maintain, and often erroneous.

We began by defining the problem. Any approach to efficient parallel computation on MIMD computers must accomplish several things:

- parallelism, if not explicitly expressed, must be exposed;

- the available parallelism must be tailored to fit the target computer;

- tasks must be assigned to processors, either statically or dynamically; and

- since tasks usually are not entirely independent, shared data must be managed.

The Par approach to parallel programming accomplishes these goals without giving up portability and clarity. The first step is to write the most natural parallel algorithm for solving a given problem. The programmer can assume that there is unlimited parallelism and that all variables are directly accessible. At this stage messy architectural details are ignored. Explicit parallelism is used because a parallel program is a clearer expression of a parallel algorithm than is a sequential program.

The initial program is refined by adding scheduling, mapping, and implementation annotations, which specialize the algorithm to the target architecture. The annotations are separated syntactically from the statement of the algorithm so that they do not obscure the algorithm and so that they can easily be changed, if necessary, for other target architectures. The original statement of the algorithm is not changed.

Adding correctly implemented annotations to a program does not affect the correctness of the program. This makes it easy to experiment with different scheduling and mapping strategies without introducing errors. Conversely, the meaning of a program does not depend on the way it is annotated; this makes it easier to understand a program or prove it correct.

We have illustrated how the Par method can be applied to a variety of algorithms. In Chapter 3 we illustrated the use of the Par method on regular algorithms. Regular algorithms allow the use of static schedulers and mappings, which can be implemented very efficiently since run-time load balancing and data management are not needed. Schedulers and mappings for regular algorithms tend to be closely interdependent. Schedulers are chosen to divide the chores evenly among the available processors. Mappings are chosen so that, for efficiency, data is stored where it is used. This leads to simple data partitioning in purely data-parallel algorithms such as matrix addition (Section 3.1), to data replication in algorithms such as matrix multiplication (Section 3.3), and to remapping in examples such as region labeling (Section 3.4).

In Chapter 4 we presented examples that showed how the Par method can be applied to irregular algorithms. Since it is impossible to predict the best assignment of chores and data to processors for such algorithms, dynamic schedulers and mapping are required for efficiency. Schedulers and mappings for irregular algorithms tend to be less closely related—and more orthogonal—than for regular algorithms. We showed how schedulers using the administrator-worker paradigm can be used to achieve load balancing. We also showed how data management techniques such as caching and generative communication can be used to ensure that most data is stored where it is used.

To support our approach to parallel programming, we have designed the Par language, which is an explicitly parallel language that supports scheduling, mapping, and implementation annotations. In Chapter 2 we introduced the Par language; in Chapter 5 we described how it can be implemented on various kinds of MIMD computers: UMA computers, NUMA computers, and multicomputers.

Finally, in Chapter 6 we contrasted the Par method with other approaches to parallel programming. We pointed out that most languages for parallel programming make a tradeoff between portability, clarity, and efficiency. At one extreme, languages that are completely architecture-independent—sequential and declarative languages, for example—are portable and clear, but current compilers for such languages cannot produce good code for many problems. At the other extreme, architecture-specific languages offer good efficiency but poor clarity and portability. The use of annotations to specify architecture-dependent details avoids this tradeoff; efficient programs can be specified without compromising clarity. And, since the annotations are separated from the rest of the program, they can be changed easily to tailor the program to a different architecture.

7.2 Application to Other Languages

We have presented our method of architecture-independent parallel programming using the Par language. However, much of our method could be adapted to other languages. Since we think it unlikely that most programmers will give up their current languages and adopt Par, we have given some thought to supporting the Par method by adapting current languages. In this section we describe a loose collection of features that could be added to any imperative language to yield a language that supports the Par method.

The essential aspects of the Par language, except for the annotations themselves, are as follows:

- some form of simple concurrent statement,

- a way to provide alternate implementations of data types, and

- facilities for programming schedulers and mappings.

A concurrent statement is necessary because the Par method begins with an explicitly parallel program. As is evident from Chapters 3 and 4, the Par method relies heavily on providing alternate implementations of data types for different computers; thus the ability to provide these alternatives is crucial. Finally, support for implementing annotations is necessary because annotations are implemented in the language, rather than somewhere "beneath" the language.

The second and third requirements are met by many object-oriented languages including, for example, C++ [110]. Thus one possibility is to add a concurrent statement and annotations to such a language. We feel that such a language would be quite workable, although perhaps less clear and elegant than the Par language.

If one is willing to give up the ability to implement annotations within the language, the requirements on the base language become much more modest. One possibility is to have a fixed collection of schedulers and mappings. These would be implemented in some language underneath the application-level language. The names of these schedulers and mappings would be used in annotations, as before. Such a system could be adapted to any imperative language: C, FORTRAN, or Pascal, for example. All that would be required would be the addition of a concurrent statement.

Although providing a fixed collection of schedulers and mappings is perhaps a workable scheme in some domains, we feel that restricting the programmer in this way will not work well in general. Schedulers and mappings are quite reusable, but we feel it unlikely that any fixed set will satisfy all programmers in all situations. The main reason for using parallel computers is speed; thus we feel that any language that seriously compromises efficiency is not likely to remain popular for long in this computational domain.

Appendix A

Partitioning Quantifiers

When writing a scheduler or mapping, it is often necessary to partition a quantifier (which represents an arithmetic sequence) among processors so that each processor receives approximately the same number of elements. Also, given such a partition, it is sometimes necessary to determine to which processor a particular element is assigned. The partition and owner functions accomplish these tasks.

For example, suppose we want to partition the quantifier

> 1 to 100 by 3

among five processors numbered 0 . . . 4. We can compute the bounds on processor p by executing

> lb, ub := partition(1, 100, 3, 5, p)

On processor 0, the bounds lb and ub will be set to 1 and 20; on processor 1 the bounds will be 22 and 40, and so forth. Thus processor 0 is assigned the quantifier

> 1 to 20 by 3

and processor 1 is assigned the quantifier

> 22 to 40 by 3

Consider first the case where $a \langle b$ and step $= 1$. This corresponds to the case where we are partitioning a sequence $\{a, a + 1, .., b\}$. We first compute size, the number of items that will be assigned to each processor:

$$\text{size} = \left\lceil \frac{b - a + 1}{n} \right\rceil$$

Then the lower and upper bounds for processor k are computed as

$$
\begin{aligned}
lb &= a + k * \text{size} \\
ub &= lb + step - 1
\end{aligned}
$$

```
proc partition(a, b, step, n, k : Int)
    size : Int := (abs(b − a) + n) div n
    delta : Int := size ∗ sign(step)
    m : Int := (k ∗ size + abs(step) − 1) div abs(step)
    lb : Int := a + m ∗ step
    ub : Int := a + (k + 1) ∗ delta − sign(step)
    if  (step > 0 and ub > b) or (step < 0 and ub < b) →
        return(lb, b)
    []  else →
        return(lb, ub)
    fi
end
```

Figure A.1: The partition function.

The situation becomes slightly more complicated when negative and non-unit values of step are allowed, but the idea is the same. Figure A.1 contains code to implement partition for general values of step.

The owner function is closely related to partition. After a quantifier has been subdivided into blocks by partition, the owner function is used to return the owner of a particular index within the range of the quantifier. In the example above, the quantifier

   1 to 100 by 3

was partitioned among 5 processors. We could determine to which processor 34 was assigned by executing

   who := owner(1, 100, 3, 5, 34)

The result will be processor 1, since processor 1 was assigned the quantifier

   22 to 40 by 3

Figure A.2 contains code for the owner function. The values of size and delta are computed as in Figure A.1; the value of owner is $\lfloor (i - a)/\text{delta} \rfloor$.

```
proc owner(a, b, step, n, i : Int)
    size : Int := abs(b − a) + n) div n
    delta : Int := size * sign(step)
    return(i − a) div delta
end
```

Figure A.2: The owner function

References

[1] ABELSON, H., ADAMS, N. L., BARTLEY, D. H., BROOKS, G., DYBVIG, R. K., FRIEDMAN, D. P., HALSTEAD, R., HANSON, C., HAYNES, C. T., KOHNBECKER, E., OXLEY, D., PITMAN, K. M., ROZAS, G. J., SUSSMAN, G. J., AND WAND, M. Revised[3] report on the algorithmic language Scheme. Available from the Artificial Intelligence Laboratory, Massachusetts Institute of Technology.

[2] ACKERMAN, W. B. AND DENNIS, J. B. *VAL—A Value-Oriented Algorithmic Language: Preliminary Reference Manual.* Laboratory for Computer Science, MIT, Cambridge, Mass., 1979.

[3] AGHA, G. Actors: A Model of Concurrent Computation in Distributed Systems. PhD dissertation, University of Michigan, 1985. Avalable as TR-844, MIT Artificial Intelligence Laboratory.

[4] AHUJA, S., CARRIERO, N., AND GELERNTER, D. Linda and friends. *Computer 19*, 8 (August 1986), 26–34.

[5] AKL, S. G. *The Design and Analysis of Parallel Algorithms.* Prentice-Hall, Englewood Cliffs, New Jersey, 1989.

[6] ALLEN, F., BURKE, M., CHARLES, P., CYTRON, R., AND FERRANTE, J. An overview of the PTRAN analysis system for multiprocessing. *The Journal of Parallel and Distributed Computing 5*, 5 (October 1988), 617–640.

[7] ALLEN, J. R. Dependence Analysis for Subscript Variables and Its Application To Program Transformations. PhD dissertation, Rice University, April, 1983.

[8] ALLEN, J. AND KENNEDY, K. PFC: A program to convert FORTRAN to parallel form. TR 82-6, Rice Univ., Houston, Tex., March, 1982.

[9] American National Standards Institute, New York. *Reference Manual for the Ada Programming Language. ANSI/MIL-STD 1815A*, January, 1983.

[10] ANDREWS, G. R. AND OLSSON, R. A. Report on the SR programming language: Version 1.1. TR 89-6, Dept. of Computer Science, Univ. of Arizona, Tucson, Arizona, May, 1989.

[11] ANDREWS, G. R., OLSSON, R. A., COFFIN, M., ELSHOFF, I., NILSEN, K., PURDIN, T., AND TOWNSEND, G. An overview of the SR language and implementation. *ACM Transactions on Programming Languages and Systems 10*, 1 (January 1988), 51–86.

[12] ARVIND, R. AND PINGALI, K.   Id Nouveau: Language and operational semantics.   CSG Memo   M.I.T., September, 1987.

[13] ATKINS, M. S. AND OLSSON, R. A.   Performance of multi-tasking and synchronization mechanisms in the programming language SR.   *Software Practice and Experience 18*, 9 (September 1988), 879–895.

[14] BACKUS, J.   1977 Turing Award Lecture: Can programming be liberated from the von Neumann style? A functional style and its algebra of programs.   *Communications of the ACM 21*, 8 (August 1978), 613–641.   Reprinted in *ACM Turing Award Lectures*, ACM Press, 1987, 63–130.

[15] BAL, H. E.   The Shared Data-object Model as a Paradigm for Programming Distributed Systems.   PhD dissertation, Vrije Universiteit of Amsterdam, 1989.

[16] BAL, H. E., STEINER, J. G., AND TANNENBAUM, A. S.   Programming languages for distributed computing systems.   *ACM Computing Surveys 21*, 3 (September 1989), 261–322.

[17] BALDWIN, D. AND QUIROZ, C.   Parallel programming and the Consul language.   In *Proceedings of the 1987 International Conference on Parallel Processing*.   389–392.

[18] BANERJEE, U.   *Dependence Analysis for Supercomputing*.   Klower Academic, 1988.

[19] BANERJEE, U.   Data dependence in ordinary programs.   Master's thesis, Univerisy of Illinois at Urbana-Champaign, November, 1976.

[20] BANERJEE, U.   Speedup of Ordinary Programs.   PhD dissertation, Univerisy of Illinois at Urbana-Champaign, October, 1979.

[21] BARENDREGT, H. P.   *The Lambda Calculus: Its Syntax and Semantics*.   Volume 103 of *Studies in Logic and The Foundations of Mathematics*, Elsevier Science Publishers B.V., 1000 BZ Amsterdam, The Netherlands, 1984.

[22] BERNSTEIN, A. J.   Analysis of programs for parallel processing.   *IEEE Transactions on Electronic Computers 15*, 5 (October 1966).

[23] BERTSEKAS, D. P. AND TSITSIKLIS, J. N.   *Parallel and Distributed Computation (Numerical Methods)*.   Prentice Hall, Englewood Cliffs, New Jersey, 1989.

[24] BOKARI, S. H.   A shortest tree algorithm for optimal assignments across space and time in a distributed processor system.   *IEEE Transactions on Software Engineering SE-7*, 6 (November 1981), 583–589.

[25] BOLOSKY, W. J. Personal correspondence, April, 1990.

[26] BOLOSKY, W. J., FITZGERALD, R. P., AND SCOTT, M. L. Simple but effective techniques for NUMA memory management. In Proceedings of the Twelfth ACM Symposium on Operating Systems Principles (Litchfield Park, Arizona, December 3–6, 1989). *Operating Systems Review 23*, 5 (1989), 19–31.

[27] BROOKS, E. D. The butterfly barrier. *International Journal of Parallel Programming 15*, 4 (August 1986), 295–307.

[28] BRYANT, R. M. AND AGRE, J. R. A queueing network approach to the module allocation problem. *Performance Evaluation Review 10*, 3 (Fall 1981), 191–204.

[29] BURKE, M. AND CYTRON, R. Interprocedural dependence analysis and parallelization. In Proceedings of the SIGPLAN '86 Symposium on Compiler Construction (Palo Alto, California, June 25–27, 1986). *SIGPLAN Notices 21*, 7 (July 1986), 162–175.

[30] BURTON, F. W. Annotations to control parallelism and reduction order in the distibuted evaluation of functional programs. *ACM Transactions on Programming Languages and Systems 6*, 2 (April 1984), 159–174.

[31] CALLAHAN, D. A Global Approach to Detection of Parallelism. PhD dissertation, Rice Univ., Houston, Tex., April, 1987.

[32] CALLAHAN, D., COOPER, K. D., KENNEDY, K., AND TORCZON, L. Advanced techniques in interprocedural analysis. COMP TR 87-48, Rice University, Houston, Texas, June, 1987.

[33] CALLAHAN, D. AND KENNEDY, K. Compiling programs for distributed-memory multiprocessors. TR 88-74, Dept. of Computer Science, Rice Univ., Houston, Texas, August, 1988.

[34] CARRIERO, N. AND GELERNTER, D. How to write parallel programs: A guide to the perplexed. *ACM Computing Surveys 21*, 3 (September 1989), 321–357.

[35] CARRIERO, N. AND GELERNTER, D. Linda in context. *Communications of the ACM 32*, 4 (April 1989), 444–458.

[36] CHANDY, K. M. AND MISRA, J. *Parallel Program Design: A Foundation.* Addison-Wesley, 1988.

[37] CHEN, M. Very-high-level parallel programming in Crystal. TR RR-506, Dept. of Computer Science, Yale Univ., New Haven, Conn., December, 1986.

[38] CHEN, M., CHEN, Y.I., AND LI, J.   Crystal: From functional description to efficient parallel code.   In *The Proceedings of the Third Conference on Hypercube Concurrent Computers and Applications* (Pasadena, California, Jan. 19–20, 1988). ACM Press, 1988, 417–433.

[39] CHEN, M. C.   A design methodology for synthesizing parallel algorithms and architectures.   *Journal of Parallel and Distributed Computing 3*, 4 (December 1986), 461–491.

[40] CHERITON, D. R.   Preliminary thoughts on problem-oriented shared memory: A decentralized approach to distributed systems.   *Operating Systems Review 19*, 4 (October 1985), 26–33.

[41] COURTOIS, P. J., HEYMANS, F., AND PARNAS, D. L.   Concurrent control with "readers" and "writers".   *Communications of the ACM 14*, 10 (October 1971), 667–668.

[42] CYTRON, R., HIND, M., AND HSIEH, W.   Automatic generation of DAG parallelism.   In SIGPLAN '89 Conference on Programming Language Design and Implementation (Portland, Oregon, June 21–23, 1989).   *SIGPLAN Notices 23*, 5 (July 1989), 54–68.

[43] DIJKSTRA, E. W.   *A Discipline of Programming*.   Prentice-Hall, Englewood Cliffs, New Jersey, 1976.

[44] DOWNEY, P. J.   Personal Correspondence, August, 1990.

[45] EFE, K.   Heuristic models of task assignment scheduling in distributed systems.   *Computer 15*, 6 (June 1982), 50–56.

[46] FELDMAN, S.   Make—a program for maintaining computer programs.   *Software Practice and Experience 9*, (1979), 255–265.

[47] FOX, A. L. AND FOWLER, R. J.   The implementation of a coherent memory abstraction on a NUMA mulitprocessor: Experiences with PLATINUM.   In Proceedings of the Twelfth ACM Symposium on Operating Systems Principles (Litchfield Park, Arizona, December 3–6, 1989).   *Operating Systems Review 23*, 5 (1989), 32–44.

[48] FOX, G., JOHNSON, M., LYZENGA, G., OTTO, S., SALMON, J., AND WALKER, D.   *Solving Problems on Concurrent Processors: General Techniques and Regular Problems*.   Volume 1, Prentice Hall, Englewood Cliffs, New Jersey, 1988.

[49] FOX, G., editor.   *The Proceedings of the Third Conference on Hypercube Concurrent Computers and Applications* (Pasadena, California, Jan. 19–20, 1988).   ACM Press, January, 1988.

[50] GELERNTER, D.   Generative communication in Linda.   *ACM Transactions on Programming Languages and Systems 7*, 1 (January 1985), 80–112.

[51] GELERNTER, D.   Multiple tuple spaces in Linda.   In *PARLE '89 Parallel Architectures and Languages Europe. Volume II: Parallel Languages.*   Springer-Verlag, 1989, 20–27.

[52] GENTLEMAN, W. M.   Message passing between sequential processes: the reply primitive and the administrator concept.   *Software Practice and Engineering 11*, (1981), 435–466.

[53] GOLDBERG, A. AND ROBSON, D.   *Smalltalk-80: The Language and its Implementation.*   Addison-Wesley, Reading, Mass., 1983.

[54] GOLDBERG, B.   Multiprocessor execution of functional programs.   *International Journal of Parallel Programming 17*, 5 (October 1988), 425–473.

[55] GUPTA, R. AND HILL, C. R.   A scalable implementation of barrier synchronization using an adaptive combining tree.   *International Journal of Parallel Programming 18*, 3 (June 1989), 161–180.

[56] HENSGEN, D., FINKEL, R., AND MANBER, U.   Two algorithms for barrier synchronization.   *International Journal of Parallel Programming 17*, 1 (February 1988), 1–18.

[57] HOARE, C.   Communicating sequential processes.   *Communications of the ACM 21*, 8 (August 1978), 666–677.

[58] HOGGER, C.   *Introduction to Logic Programming.*   Volume 21 of *APIC Studies in Data Processing*, Academic Press, 1984.

[59] HUDAK, P.   Denotational semantics of a para-functional programming language.   *International Journal of Parallel Programming 15*, 2 (April 1986), 103–125.

[60] HUDAK, P.   Para-functional programming.   *Computer 19*, 8 (August 1986), 60–69.

[61] HUDAK, P.   Exploring parafunctional programming: Separating the what from the how.   *IEEE Software 5*, 1 (January 1988), 54–88.

[62] HUDAK, P.   Concepts, evolution, and applications of functional programming.   *ACM Computing Surveys 21*, 3 (September 1989), 359–411.

[63] HUDAK, P., WADLER, P., ARVIND, , BOUTEL, B., FAIRBAIRN, J., FASEL, J., HAMMOND, K., HUGHS, J., JOHNSSON, T., KIEBURTZ, D., NIKHIL, R., JONES, S. P., REEVE, M., WISE, D., AND YOUNG, J.   Report on the programming language Haskell.   RR 777, Yale University, New Haven, Connecticut, April, 1990.

[64] HUTCHINSON, N. C., RAJ, R. K., BLACK, A. P., LEVY, H. M., AND JUL, E. The Emerald programming language report. TR 87-29, Dept. of Computer Science, Univ. of Arizona, Tucson, Ariz., October, 1987.

[65] IVERSON, K. *A Programming Language.* Wiley, New York, 1962.

[66] JORDAN, H. F., BENTEN, M. S., ARENSTORF, N. S., AND RAMANAN, A. V. *Force Users Manual.* Department of Electrical and Computer Engineering, Univ. of Colorado, Boulder, Colorado, June, 1987.

[67] KARP, A. H. Programming for parallelism. *Computer 20*, 5 (May 1987), 43–57.

[68] KENNEDY, K. Automatic translation of FORTRAN programs to vector form. TR 476-029-4, Rice University, October, 1980.

[69] KERNIGHAN, B. W. AND RICHIE, D. M. *The C Programming Language.* Prentice-Hall, Inc., Englewood Cliffs, New Jersey, 1978.

[70] KNUTH, D. E. *The Art of Computer Programming.* Volume 3, Addison-Wesley, 1973.

[71] KOELBEL, C. Personal Correspondence, May, 1990.

[72] KOELBEL, C. AND MEHROTRA, P. Supporting shared data structures on distributed memory architectures. In *Second ACM SIGPLAN Symposium on Principles and Practice of Parallel Programming* Seattle, Washington, March 14–16, 1990). *SIGPLAN Notices 25*, 3 (March 1990), 177–186.

[73] KOELBEL, C., MEHROTRA, P., AND ROSENDALE, J. V. Semi-automatic domain decomposition in BLAZE. In *Proceedings of the 1987 International Conference on Parallel Processing.* 521–524.

[74] KOWALSKI, R. *Logic for Problem Solving.* North Holland, 1979.

[75] LAKSHMIVARAHAN, S. AND DHALL, S. K. *Analysis and Design of Parallel Algorithms.* McGraw-Hill, 1990.

[76] LEASURE, B. Compiling serial languages for parallel machines. TR 78-805, Univerisity of Illinois at Urbana-Champaign, November, 1976.

[77] LI, K. Shared Virtual Memory on Loosely Coupled Multiprocessors. PhD dissertation, Yale Univ., September, 1986.

[78] LI, Z., YEW, P.-C., AND ZHU, C.-Q. An efficient data dependence analysis for parallelizing compilers. *IEEE Transactions on Parallel and Distributed Systems 1*, 1 (January 1990), 26–34.

[79] LIEBERMAN, H. Concurrent object oriented programming in Act 1. In YONEZAWA, A. AND TOKORO, , editors, *Concurrent Object Oriented Programming*. MIT Press, Cambridge, Mass., 1986.

[80] LIEBERMAN, H. Using prototypical objects to implement shared behavior in object oriented systems. In *Object-Oriented Programming Systems, Languages, and Applications: Conference Proceedings*. ACM, 11 West 42nd Street, New York, New York 10036, 1986, 214–223, Special issue of *SIGPLAN Notices 21* (11), Nov. 1986.

[81] LISKOV, B. Distributed programming in Argus. *Communications of the ACM 31*, 3 (March 1988), 300–312.

[82] MACE, M. E. *Memory Storage Patterns in Parallel Processing*. The Kluwer International Series in Engineering and Computer Science, Kluwer Academic Publishers, 101 Philip Drive, Assinippi Park, Norwell, Mass., 1987. PhD dissertation.

[83] MATSUOKA, S. AND KAWAI, S. Using tuple-space communication in distributed object-oriented languages. In *Proc. Object-Oriented Programming Systems, Languages, and Applications*. ACM Press, 1988, 276–284.

[84] MCGRAW, J., SKEDZIELEWSKI, S., ALLAN, S., OLDEHOEFT, R., GLAUERT, J., KIRKHAM, C., NOYCE, B., AND THOMAS, R. SISAL: Streams and iteration in a single assignment language. Manual 146, Lawrence Livermore National Laboratory, Livermore, Cal., March, 1985.

[85] MCGRAW, J. R. The VAL language: Description and analysis. *ACM Transactions on Programming Languages and Systems 4*, 1 (January 1982), 44–82.

[86] MEHROTRA, P. AND ROSENDALE, J. V. The BLAZE language: A parallel language for scientific programming. TR 85-29, ICASE, Hampton, Virginia, 1987. To appear in *Parallel Computing*.

[87] MEYER, B. *Object-oriented Software Construction*. Prentice Hall International Series in Computer Science, Prentice Hall, Hertfordshire, Great Britain, 1988.

[88] MORISON, R. AND OTTO, S. W. The scattered decomposition for finite element problems. *Journal of Scientific Computing 2*, (1986).

[89] MYERS, E. W. A precise inter-procedural data flow algorithm. In *Conference Record of the Eighth Annual ACM Symposium on Principles of Programming Languages* (Williamsburg, Virginia, Jan. 26–28, 1981). ACM Press, 1981, 219–230.

[90] NICOL, D. M., SALZ, J. H., AND TOWNSEND, J. C.   Delay point schedules for irregular parallel computations.   *International Journal of Parallel Programming 18*, 3 (February 1989), 69–90.

[91] OLSSON, R. A. AND WHITEHEAD, G. R.   A simple technique for automatic recompilation in modular programming languages.   *Software Practice and Experience 19*, 8 (August 1989), 757–773.

[92] PARR, F. N. AND STROM, R. E.   NIL: A high-level language for distributed systems programming.   *IBM Systems Journal 22*, 1/2 (1983), 111–127.

[93] REES, J. A., ADAMS, N. I., AND MEEHAN, J. R.   *The T Manual*.   Computer Science Dept., Yale Univ., New Haven, CT, January, 1984.

[94] ROBERT H. HALSTEAD, J.   Multilisp: A language for concurrent symbolic computation.   *ACM Transactions on Programming Languages and Systems 7*, 4 (October 1985), 501–538.

[95] ROBERT H. HALSTEAD, J.   An assessment of Multilisp: Lessons from experience.   *International Journal of Parallel Programming 15*, 6 (December 1986), 459–501.

[96] ROBERT H. HALSTEAD, J.   Parallel symbolic computing.   *IEEE Computer 19*, 8 (August 1986), 35–43.

[97] ROGERS, A. AND PINGALI, K.   Process decomposition through locality of reference.   TR 88-935, Cornell Univ., Ithaca, NY, August, 1988.   Submitted to Third Symposium on Architectural Support for Programming Languages and Operating Systems.

[98] ROSING, M., SCHNABEL, R. B., AND WEAVER, R.   Dino: Summary and examples.   In *The Proceedings of the Third Conference on Hypercube Concurrent Computers and Applications* (Pasadena, California, Jan. 19–20, 1988).   ACM Press, 1988, 472–481.

[99] SABOT, G. W.   An Architecture-Independent Model for Parallel Programming.   PhD dissertation, Harvard Univ., Cambridge, Mass., February, 1988.

[100] SAHNI, S. K., editor.   *Proceedings of the 1987 International Conference on Parallel Processing*, Univ. Park, Penn., August, 1987. Penn. State Univ.

[101] SALTZ, J. H. AND CHEN, M. C.   Automated problem mapping: The Crystal runtime system.   RR 510, Dept. of Computer Science, Yale Univ., New Haven, Conn., January, 1987.

[102] SARASWAT, V. A.   Concurrent Constraint Programming Languages.   PhD dissertation, Carnegie-Mellon University, January, 1989.

[103] SCHEURICH, C. AND DUBOIS, M.   Dynamic page migration in multiprocessors with distributed global memory.   In *Proceedings: The 8th International Conference on Distributed Computing Systems* (San Jose, California, June 13–17, 1988).   Computer Society Press, 1730 Massachusetts Avenue, N.W., Washington D.C, 1988, 162–169.

[104] SIGOPS (ACM).   Proceedings of the Twelfth ACM Symposium on Operating Systems Principles (Litchfield Park, Arizona, December 3–6, 1989), *Operating Systems Review 23*, 5 (1989).

[105] SINCLAIR, J. B.   Efficient computation of optimal assignments for distributed tasks.   *Journal of Parallel And Distributed Computing 4*, (1987), 342–362.

[106] SINCLAIR, J. B. AND LU, M.   Module assignment in distributed systems. In *Proceeding of the 1984 Computer Networking Symposium* (Gaithersburg, Maryland, Dec. 1984).   105–111.

[107] SLADE, S.   *The T Programming Language*.   Prentice-Hall, Inc., Englewood Cliffs, NJ, 1987.

[108] SNYDER, L.   Type architectures, shared memory and the corollary of modest potential.   Type Architectures, Shared Memory and the Corollary of Modest Potential 35, Univ. of Wash., Seattle, Wash., 1986?   To appear in Annual Review of Computer Science, Vol. 1, 1986.

[109] STROM, R. E. AND YEMINI, S.   NIL: an integrated language and system for distributed programming.   *SIGPLAN Notices 18*, 6 (June 1983), 73–82.

[110] STROUSTRUP, B.   *The C++ Programming Language*.   Addison-Wesley, Reading, Mass., 1987.

[111] SUSSMAN, G. J. AND GUY LEWIS STEELE, J.   Scheme: An interpreter for extended lambda calculus.   Artificial Intelligence Memo 349, MIT, December, 1975.

[112] SWINEHART, D. C., XELLWEGER, P. T., AND HAGAMANN, R. B.   The structure of Cedar.   In *Proceedings of the ACM SIGPLAN '85 Symposium on Language Issues in Programming Environments* (Seattle, WA, July 1985).   *SIGPLAN Notices 20*, 7 (1985), 230–244.

[113] TURNER, D. A.   Miranda: A non strict functional language with polymorphic types.   In *Proceedings of the IFIP International Conference on Functional Programming Languages and Computer Architecture*.   Springer-Verlag, 1985.

[114] ULLMAN, J. D.   Polynomial complete scheduling problems.   *Operating Systems Review 7*, 4 (1973), 96–101.

[115] ULLMAN, J. D.   NP-complete scheduling problems.   In EDWARD G. COFF-MAN, J., editor, *Computer & Job/Shop Scheduling Theory*, chapter 4, 139–164. John Wiley and Son, Inc., 1976.

[116] WOLFE, M. J.   Optimizing supercompilers for supercomputers.   UIUCDCS-R 82-1105, University of Illinois at Urbana-Champaign, October, 1982.

[117] YOKOTE, Y. AND TOKORO, M.   Concurrent programming in Concurrent-Smalltalk.   In *Proceedings, Object-Oriented Programming Systems, Languages, and Applications* (Portland, Oregon, Nov. 1986).   *SIGPLAN Notices 21*, 11 (November 1986), 331–340.

[118] YOKOTE, Y. AND TOKORO, M.   Experience and evolution of Concurrent-Smalltalk.   In *Proceedings, Object-Oriented Programming Systems, Languages, and Applications* (Orlando, Florida, Dec. 1987).   *SIGPLAN Notices 21*, 12 (December 1987), 406–415.

Index